# Amateur Radio Explained

## *A Guide to Getting Started in Ham Radio*

# Ian Poole, G3YWX

**Radio Society of Great Britain**

Published by the Radio Society of Great Britain, Cranborne Road, Potters Bar, Herts EN6 3JE.


First published 2000, Second edition 2007

ISBN: 9781-9050-8632-0

*Publisher's note*

The opinions expressed in this book are those of the author and not necessarily those of the RSGB. While the information presented is believed to be correct, the author, the publisher and their agents cannot accept responsibility for consequences arising from any inaccuracies or omissions.

Production: Mark Allgar, M1MPA
Cover design: Dorotea Vizer, M3VZR
Editing, typography and design: Steve Telenius-Lowe, 9M6DXX


Printed in Great Britain by Latimer Trend

Front cover picture: Mark Haynes, M0DXR, demonstrating amateur radio at GB50, the Queen's Golden Jubilee special event station at Windsor Castle in 2002 (© RSGB).

# Contents

# Preface

I T IS SOME YEARS now since I first started short wave listening, and then obtained my amateur radio licence. Yet despite the length of time I have been interested in amateur radio I still find new areas of interest. I have also made many friends through the hobby. Some I talk to over the air whilst I meet others from time to time. It also gave me a good introduction to my career in electronics.

As you read this book, I hope that I am able to convey something of the fascination of the hobby, and the way in which it has interested me over the years. To this day I still remember the excitement of making my first contact, and then some months later the first contact, early in the morning, with the west coast of the USA. Even now I find it amazing that signals can travel over these vast distances.

In the intervening years since I gained my licence, many changes have occurred and the licence has been opened up in a way that allows many more people to be able to transmit on the amateur bands. There have also been many changes in the technology used. Valves, which were in their last throws of being used in the sixties and early seventies, have given way to transistors [except generally for high-power amplifiers – *Ed*], while in their turn transistors have often been superseded by integrated circuits. The use of much more advanced technology has allowed much greater levels of equipment sophistication and ease of operation, as well as enabling many new communications technologies to be used. This has all increased the interest level within the hobby.

I hope that I have been able to reflect some of my enthusiasm for, and fascination with, the hobby, and that the book contains the essence of this enthralling hobby. Certainly this has been my aim.

In writing the book, I have had much help from Alun Cross, G4WGE, who has checked many areas of the book and made many helpful suggestions. Also Steve Telenius-Lowe, 9M6DXX, who in undertaking the editing, typography and design made many useful suggestions and supplied a number of images. My thanks are due to both for their inputs.

*Ian Poole, G3YWX,*
*May 2007*

# 1. An Introduction to Amateur Radio

**A**MATEUR RADIO IS a unique hobby that captivates the interest of millions of people around the world today. It encompasses a wide variety of subjects, from historical aspects right up to today's latest technology. It appeals to people of all ages, from the person in the street to politicians, kings and queens. While it is a technical hobby, there is also plenty of human contact because it is all about communication. Radio amateurs, or hams as they are sometimes known, can make many friends through the hobby – some may be on the other side of town but others may be on the other side of the world.

## ABOUT THE HOBBY

There are many areas of interest and activity that are encompassed within amateur radio. Some radio amateurs will enjoy certain activities whereas others will get involved in different aspects. All of this brings a tremendous amount of variety into the hobby.

For many years, one of the main attractions has been the possibility of hearing or contacting someone many thousands of miles away. In fact many people enjoy what is called 'DXing', where they seek out stations far away or in interesting locations. Some people have stations with large antennas and sophisticated equipment with which they can regularly make contacts with stations on all continents. For those who may not want to spend as much there is no reason why they cannot take part in the action as well. With a little skill and cunning it is possible to make contact with people from many different areas of the globe with quite simple and inexpensive equipment. This makes it a hobby that is open to all.

Even though many people think of the short-wave bands as the place where radio hams can be found, this is not the full story. There are amateur bands on a variety of different frequencies. Several can be found on the short-wave bands, but there is also one just below the long-wave broadcast band, and others on the VHF and UHF bands and at higher frequencies. This adds further variety because the challenges of using the various frequencies are all different.

While operating equipment forms a large part of amateur radio, many people enjoy constructing their own. This is true even today when so much commercially-made equipment is available. Although home-built equipment is usually much simpler than that produced commercially, it is still possible to use it to make interesting contacts, and there is an enormous sense of achievement when it works and the first contact is made.

There are other aspects. At certain times of the year the bands come alive when thousands of stations come on air to participate in some of the organised contests. These can be great fun to enter.

Also, some people enjoy operating from interesting locations. These expeditions, commonly known as 'DXpeditions', attract a great deal of interest on the bands and some may

An amateur radio station.

A home-built station.

A QSL card from a DXpedition.

make many thousands of contacts in a few days. These expeditions are hard work but they can be most enjoyable.

Another part of amateur radio that has grown over the years is collecting QSL cards. These are postcard-sized cards that are often exchanged to confirm that a contact took place. They can be very colourful, often having photographs of the country of origin, and they provide an interesting record of the places that have been contacted. Nowadays with the advent of the Internet and e-mail, electronic 'cards' are also being sent, but the original paper-based cards still remain very popular.

It is also possible to collect awards. These can be gained for a variety of operating challenges. One

of the most famous is called the DX Century Club or 'DXCC' and is gained for submitting proof of making contact with at least 100 countries. These awards provide challenges that add further interest to operating on the various amateur bands and the awards themselves can be very attractive.

Computer technology is playing an increasingly important role in the hobby. Not only are there many amateur radio related computer programs that carry out important tasks like station logging, predicting radio propagation conditions and the like, but it is also possible to link a computer to the transmitter and receiver and communicate over radio using the computers. Early data communications used large, heavy teleprinters.

Now computers are able to provide error-resilient systems with considerable degrees of flexibility that ensure amateur radio is truly in the computer age.

Amateur radio is also not only about enjoying yourself. In many areas it helps the community and on many occasions it has helped to save lives. It is an unfortunate fact of life that disasters strike from time to time, and often in these situations communications need to be set up swiftly, sometimes under very difficult conditions. Radio amateurs are uniquely placed to help at times like these. Having the equipment available, the knowledge required to set up a station, and the enthusiasm to help, they can provide a life-saving service. On many occasions amateur radio has provided the only means of communications from a hurricane-hit island because all the normal communications systems have been put out of action. In the UK as well radio amateurs provide significant levels of help and many groups using the banner Raynet® have been set up. Raynet® groups frequently run exercises to ensure a high state of readiness.

For those looking for a career, amateur radio can provide an excellent starting place. Many electronic development engineers started by having an interest in amateur radio. This stood them in good stead for further education. It is also a fact that many employers look for radio amateurs because they are known to have

A DXpedition in operation.

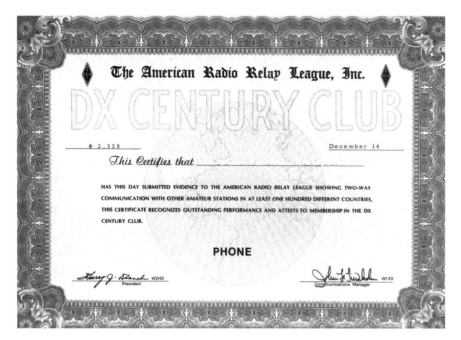

The DX Century Club certificate.

good practical experience in radio and electronics.

## LICENCES
Having listened on the amateur bands, many people will want to be able to transmit. The amateur radio licence allows many privileges and a great deal of flexibility. For example, radio amateurs are allowed to use high powers (very much higher than CB for example) and they are able to use equipment they have constructed or designed themselves.

As a result, a degree of technical competence is required and so to gain an amateur radio licence it is necessary to pass some tests. These vary according to the country and type of licence required. All licences require the applicant to sit a theory examination, and some require a Morse test to be passed.

Whilst these may seem daunting to the newcomer, many millions of people have successfully managed to gain their licences, and a large proportion of them did not have a technical background.

## HOW IT STARTED
Amateur radio has been in existence since the very beginnings of radio it-self. Maxwell, a great theoretician, postulated the existence of radio waves and then Heinrich Hertz was the first to demonstrate them. Later Marconi performed many experiments with these new 'Hertzian' waves, improving greatly the distances over which they could be detected. He believed they could be used for communicating over long distances and accordingly set up his own company to do so. In his efforts to advertise his company he gave many lectures and talks and set new transmitting distance records. These captured the imagination of many people. Stories hit the newspapers, and this started a growing interest in the subject. Some hobby magazines at the time started to publish designs for making the equipment to study these new 'wireless' waves.

One person who heard a talk by Marconi was named M J C Dennis. His imagination was captured by the subject, and he decided to set up his own station. This he did in 1898 at Woolwich Arsenal. He did not have a commercial interest in the subject and accordingly this was the first truly amateur radio station.

A number of other people followed in his footsteps as interest grew and more amateur experimental stations were set up. In these very early days no licences were required, but in 1904 the UK Wireless Telegraphy Act became law and people were required to obtain a licence before transmitting. Fortunately the act was interpreted favourably for amateur experimenters and the popularity of the hobby grew. However, it was not easy in these days. Very few ready-made components were available, and certainly no ready-made equipment. Interest continued to grow until the outbreak of the First World War when all licences were revoked in the UK and equipment was impounded.

After the war activity started again. This time amateur experimenters were soon relegated from the long wavelengths that were used at this time for long-distance communications. They were given the short-wave bands which were thought to be relatively unimportant. However, American stations soon reported making long-distance contacts and this raised the possibility of making a trans-Atlantic contact on the short-wave bands.

After several attempts the first contact was made between a French station and one in New England and this was on a wavelength of around 100 metres (a frequency of about 3MHz). Soon after this more contacts were made between Europe and

An early amateur radio station.

North America, and shortly afterwards contact was made between a British station and one in New Zealand. Against all the odds, radio amateurs had proved the worth of the short-wave bands.

Technology improved in the 1920s and '30s, and radio amateurs played a vital role in developing it and discovering more about the way in which radio waves travelled. However, in 1939 the Second World War broke out and activity ceased in most countries, including the UK. Nevertheless, radio amateurs played a key role and used their skills for the war effort.

Activity recommenced shortly after the war. The new UK licence had fewer restrictions than previously, and soon even more facilities were allowed. Shortly afterwards mobile operation and amateur television were permitted and new frequency bands were allocated. These all gave rise to new challenges.

Again radio amateurs found their contributions were invaluable in many areas. Even so, people looked to amateur radio more as a relaxing pastime. More commercially-made equipment became available, initially from the UK and the USA, but towards the end of the 1960s, sets from Japan started to appear on the market. Mobile operation increased with the greater use of the VHF and UHF bands and the wider availability of mobile and hand-held equipments for these frequencies.

## THE HOBBY TODAY AND TOMORROW

Despite the enormous changes that have taken place in technology over the last few years, there will always be a place for amateur radio. Indeed, many of these new developments *increase* interest in the hobby. Amateur satellites have been launched and there has also been operation from space missions, both American and Russian. In addition to this, new methods of data transmission have been devised that are far more efficient.

An amateur radio satellite.

Computer technology is being used even more widely. New forms of communication are being researched and devised, and computers are being used to act as digital signal processors where some of the functions of the radio are being undertaken by the computer. Computer technology in the form of the Internet is also having an impact on the hobby. Not only are there many amateur radio related web sites, but it is also possible to access parts of the Internet via amateur radio transmissions.

For the future there will be many more exciting technological developments that radio amateurs will use for their hobby. In the past the pioneering spirit of radio amateurs has

Amateur radio operation from the Russian space station *Mir*.

paved the way. In the future there is no doubt that amateur radio will use new technology and in some areas it will help to discover or define new aspects of technology. It will always be great fun, and it is likely that there will be more variety in the way you can be involved and enjoy the hobby. It is certainly a pastime that will captivate you for life, providing interest, friends and enjoyment.

A data communications station.

# 2. Types of Transmission

Photo: 9M6DXX

A straight Morse key and a paddle used with an electronic Morse keyer.

**A**NYONE USING a short-wave receiver will quickly realise there are very many different types of transmission. Sometimes signals will be heard using the Morse code, while at other times voices or music may be heard or even a variety of different types of indecipherable sounds. All of these noises are being used to carry information of one kind or another. Some of it may be broadcast information, other may be short messages to and from ships, and others may be carrying various forms of data, such as computer-style data. Even when transmissions are carrying audio information there are a number of different ways in which this can be done. Some methods are better in some circumstances whereas other types are better in others.

## CARRIERS AND MODULATION

A radio signal can be thought of as having two constituents. The first is called the *carrier* and this is the steady-state radio signal that is not carrying any information in the way of data, speech or whatever. It is simply the signal that is created by an oscillator circuit and transmitted or radiated. For it to carry useful information, *modulation* must be applied. This changes or modifies the signal in some way and there are several ways of doing this. Some are very simple but others used for some of the new forms of transmission like digital radio become very compli-

cated. Fortunately those that are widely used in amateur radio are quite straightforward.

## MORSE CODE

The simplest type of transmission is a Morse transmission. This simply consists of a carrier wave that is switched on and off to make the 'dots' and 'dashes', as shown in **Fig 2.1**.

Although the Morse code was devised in the mid-nineteenth century and used for wire telegraph messages, it lent itself particularly well

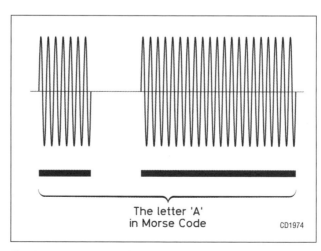

The letter 'A'
in Morse Code
CD1974

**Fig 2.1. A Morse code signal.**

to being used over radio. In the early days, when technology was very basic, Morse was the only way of communicating via radio. Even when it became possible to modulate signals with speech or music, it was still widely used. Today it is only necessary to tune across the short-wave bands to hear that it is still being used extensively. The reason for this is simply that it has some advantages over other modes. The prime reason is that it is much easier to 'read' a Morse signal when it is very weak than any other type of transmission.

A further advantage that is particularly useful for radio amateurs is that the equipment required to transmit a Morse signal is very simple. It can be relatively easy to build a Morse transmitter, and indeed one can even be built using a single tran-

**An electronic Morse keyer.**

sistor.

The disadvantage of a Morse transmission is that in order to receive it a *beat frequency oscillator* (BFO) is required in many types of receiver. Without a BFO the incoming signal would sound like a series of thumps and clicks, whereas when one is used it enables the Morse signal to have the characteristic 'bleeping' tone. Receivers that are to be used for the short-wave bands usually have a BFO that can be switched in and out as appropriate.

## AMPLITUDE MODULATION (AM)

The most obvious form of modulation is *amplitude modulation* (AM). Here the actual size or *amplitude* of the signal is varied in line with the volt-age of the modulating waveform. In other words, if the audio signal consists of a sine wave, then the radio frequency signal will vary in line with the audio signal as shown in **Fig 2.2**.

When a signal is modulated, *sidebands* are produced. If the modulating signal is a 1kHz tone, two other signals appear 1kHz either side of the main carrier. If the tone is replaced by speech or music that consists of a whole variety of different sounds at different frequencies, signals are seen either side of the carrier as shown in **Fig 2.3**.

Unfortunately amplitude modulation is not a very efficient method of transmission. It can be seen from the diagram that it takes up twice the bandwidth of the audio signal and it does not use the transmitted power very efficiently either. However, its advantage is that it is very easy to extract the audio from the signal in the receiver.

AM is mainly used for broadcast transmissions on the long, medium and short-wave bands, and also by aircraft above 108MHz. Other modes are used in preference by amateurs because they give better performance.

## SINGLE SIDEBAND

Single sideband (SSB) is widely used on the short-wave bands by professionals and amateurs. It offers a number of advantages which include:

• It occupies less valuable space on the bands;
• It uses the transmitted power more efficiently than AM.

A single sideband signal is a derivative of amplitude modulation. As the carrier itself does not contribute to conveying the modulation, it is removed. Its actual purpose is to provide a reference signal for the demodulation process and it can be

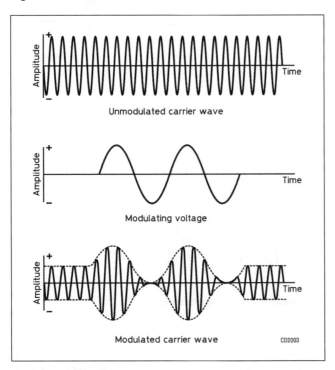

**Fig 2.2. Amplitude modulation of a carrier wave by a single sine wave.**

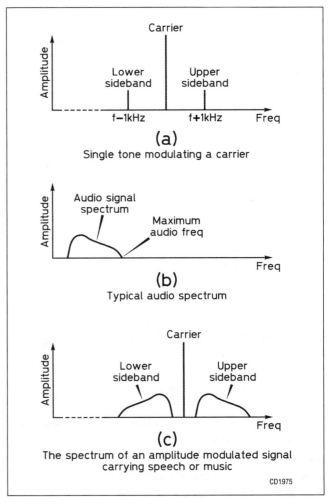

**Fig 2.3. Spectrum of an amplitude modulated signal.**

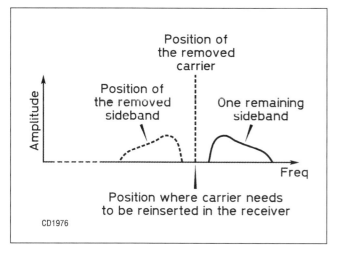

Fig 2.4. Spectrum of a single sideband signal.

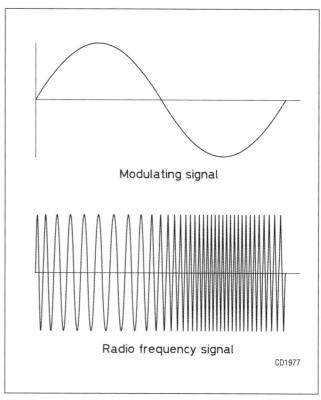

Modulating signal

Radio frequency signal

Fig 2.5. Frequency modulation.

regenerated locally in the receiver. Also, the two sidebands are virtually identical, the only difference being that one is a mirror image of the other. One of these can be removed, to halve the amount of bandwidth that is taken up by the signal, without any detrimental effects. This leaves only one sideband. If this is received on an ordinary broadcast set capable of receiving AM the signal will sound very garbled. To reconvert this back into intelligible audio a beat frequency oscillator (BFO) and mixer are required in the demodulation process. Often the mixer is called a *product detector* when used in this application, and the BFO may be called a *carrier insertion oscillator* (CIO).

As it is possible to use either sideband equally well, there is a convention for radio amateurs that the upper sideband (USB) is used on frequencies above 10MHz and the lower sideband (LSB) is used on frequencies below 10MHz.

When a single sideband signal is received the BFO or CIO must be switched on and its signal must be set to replace the carrier as shown in **Fig 2.4**. Any mismatch in frequency will cause the pitch of the reconstituted audio to change. A frequency offset of less than 100Hz is usually tolerable for most communications applications, and this can normally be achieved quite easily with a modern communications receiver.

## FREQUENCY MODULATION

Instead of varying the *amplitude* of a signal as in AM it is also possible to vary the *frequency* in line with the modulating signal. In some circumstances this has a number of advantages over amplitude modulation and as a result it is used to carry the high-quality broadcast transmissions on the VHF band. It is also used for point-to-point and mobile transmissions such as those used by taxis and the like. Similarly, radio amateurs use FM extensively on the VHF and UHF bands for mobile and other relatively local communications.

When frequency modulating a carrier, the incoming audio waveform is made to vary the frequency of the transmission as shown in **Fig 2.5**.

In this way the *amplitude* of the transmission remains constant and only the frequency varies. When demodulating the signal to provide the audio in the receiver, the circuit must be frequency sensitive so that it changes the frequency variations back into voltage changes that can be passed into the audio amplifier and then into a loudspeaker or headphones. As it is only the frequency variations that carry the information, the levels of noise and interference that predominantly appear as amplitude variations can be ignored. Also fading and level changes have considerably less effect. This means that noise levels are reduced and signal variations like those experienced in moving cars have considerably less effect.

The amount by which the frequency changes is called the *deviation*. This may be small, typically ±3kHz in the case of many point-to-point and amateur transmissions. This is known as *narrow-band FM* (NBFM) as it only occupies a relatively narrow bandwidth.

Broadcast transmissions have a comparatively large level of deviation, typically ±75kHz, and this is known as *wide-band FM*. Obviously, the larger the deviation, the wider the bandwidth the transmission occupies - these transmissions occupy about 200kHz - but there are also improvements in the audio quality of the transmission.

## RADIO TELETYPE

Apart from sending messages by Morse code or using audio, it is also possible to send data messages, usually text. The earliest type of data transmission was known as radio teletype (RTTY). Originally teleprinters - large, noisy mechanical machines - were required to print out or generate the data but today computers can do this job and are far more convenient and pleasant to use.

The data is modulated on to the carrier using a system known as *frequency shift keying* (FSK). This type of modulation involves changing the frequency of the carrier between two different frequencies. By using a beat frequency oscillator in the receiver the shift in the carrier frequency produces two audio tones. However, the receiver does need to be tuned relatively accurately so that the tones that are produced are within the requirements of the system.

When used with VHF or UHF transmissions (those on frequencies above 30MHz) a system known as audio frequency shift keying (AFSK) is employed. This type of modulation involves modulating the carrier (generally using FM) with an audio tone. This audio tone is then shifted between the two frequencies.

Using this system the receiver tuning becomes far less critical and this is more suitable for use at frequencies in the VHF portion of the spectrum and above, where receiver stability can be a problem.

## PACKET RADIO

Radio teletype is an early form of data transmission which suffers from interference and transmits data slowly. With the rise of computer technology, new forms of transmission are available. One of the most popular is known as *packet radio* and can be found chiefly on the VHF and UHF bands.

As the name suggests, data is sent in 'packets' or short bursts and, once successfully received, the sta-tion with whom contact is being made sends back an acknowledgement to this effect. If an error is detected, a request to re-send the data packet will be made. In this way a complete message consisting of a number of packets of data can be sent and received without errors being displayed at the receiving end.

Apart from the ability to send messages with a negligible number of errors, packet offers many other advantages. A mailbox system similar to e-mail is employed. Messages can be sent to other radio amateurs (but since radio is used there are no telephone charges).

In addition to this there is a *bulletin board system* (BBS). This is similar to the news groups on the World Wide Web where information is posted for people to access.

## AMTOR AND PSK31

Although packet radio is the most widely used form of data communication on the VHF and UHF bands, other modes are preferred on the HF bands (below 30MHz). The reason for this is that the packets of data are relatively long and the much higher levels of interference and fading at HF mean that it is less successful.

As a result, a mode known as AmTOR (*Amateur Telex Over Radio*) has been developed. The way in which AmTOR works is somewhat different to packet. Groups of three letters are sent, and after each group the receiver checks to ensure it has received them correctly. If so it sends an acknowledgement to the transmitter which sends the next three letters. This mode is used when in contact with another station and is known as 'Mode A'.

When sending out general messages to several stations the method is changed slightly to what is known as 'Mode B'. Letters are sent twice with a small interval between them in case any noise crackles are present.

In addition to AmTOR, a large number of advanced data modes are now being used. Many of these take advantage of the processing power of computers, and often all that is required in addition to the basic radio transceiver and computer is a sound card for the PC, and software that is often freely available on the Internet.

These new data modes often enable the number of errors to be reduced either by reconstituting the corrupted data or asking for that packet to be re-sent. They also include other performance enhancements to ensure the data is transmitted with the minimum number of errors and as swiftly as possible. One such system that has gained considerable popularity is known as PSK31 and this mode is particularly good at providing copy when signal levels are very low.

## TELEVISION (FAST AND SLOW SCAN)

The amateur radio licence allows the transmission of two types of television signals. The most obvious is the fast-scan system that is used for normal analogue broadcast transmissions. However, as this takes up a lot of spectrum space (typically about 6MHz), it is normally only found on bands above 430MHz. The standards used for this are broadly the same as those used for broadcast transmission and this means that ordinary televisions can be used, greatly reducing the cost of any equipment that is bought and used.

See **Fig 2.6**. The system operates by scanning an image. The light

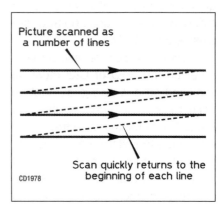

Fig 2.6. Scanning a picture.

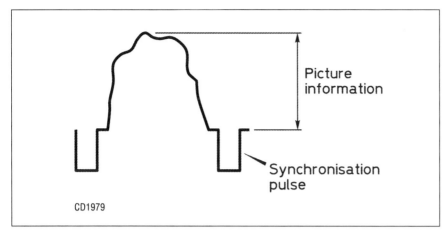

**Fig 2.7. A television signal.**

level at each point is detected and so a representation of the image can be transmitted. At the receiver a similar point is scanned and this reproduces the level of light at the transmitter. In this way a representation of the picture can be built up.

Obviously it is important that the transmitter and receiver are synchronised, and this is achieved using synchronisation pulses that are inserted at the beginning of each line and frame, as shown in **Fig 2.7**. This signal is then modulated on to a carrier.

For bands that are lower in frequency a system known as *slow-scan television* (SSTV) is used. This system uses up much less spectrum space or bandwidth but some of the advantages of the wide-band fast-scan television are lost, for instance the ability to transmit *moving* pictures. Even so, SSTV provides a very useful way of sending pictures around the world.

The system operates in basically the same way as a fast-scan television system using a scanning system. However, the rate at which pictures are scanned is much slower and the number of lines is less. The normal standard for a picture is 120 or 128 lines a frame and it may take around eight seconds to send. To transmit a slow-scan television signal the standard is to use an audio tone that is varied in pitch according to the light level. This is modulated on to a single sideband signal. An

audio frequency of 1200Hz is used for a frame pulse, 1500Hz for black and up to 2300Hz for peak white.

## SIMPLEX AND DUPLEX

A *simplex* transmission occurs when two stations are in contact and one is transmitting whilst the other is listening. Transmission has to be handed over from one station to the other, and communication is only possible in one direction at any moment. Simplex operation only requires the use of one frequency and is used by many point-to-point and mobile services like taxis. It is also the way

in which radio amateurs communicate.

To create a more natural form of communication it is necessary to have communication in both directions at once. This can only be achieved by having stations transmitting and receiving simultaneously. This type of system is known as *duplex* (**Fig 2.8**). Obviously the transmitter and receiver must be on different frequencies, and the separation must be such that the transmitter does not interfere with the receiver in the same station. Duplex operation is used for mobile telephones.

**FURTHER INFORMATION**
*Radio Communication Handbook*, 8th edn, Mike Dennison, G3XDV, and Chris Lorek, G4HCL (eds), RSGB, 2005.
*Guide to VHF/UHF Amateur Radio*, Ian Poole, G3YWX, RSGB, 2000.
*Newnes Guide to Radio and Communications Technology*, Ian Poole, Newnes (imprint of Elsevier).

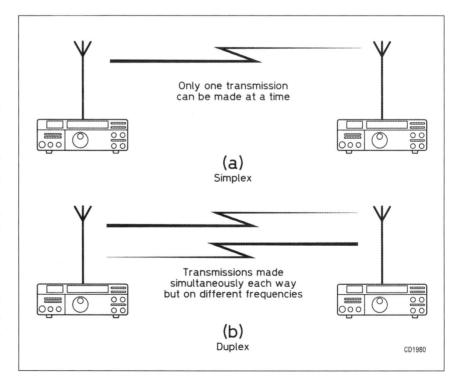

**Fig 2.8. Simplex and duplex operation.**

# 3. What You Can Hear

ANYONE TUNING THE radio spectrum with a general-coverage receiver will be able to hear an enormous variety of signals. Some will carry sounds such as speech or music, whereas many others may appear as strange noises, and these can be carrying other forms of modulation that may be data, pictures, faxes and a whole variety of other transmissions. These may be coming from almost anywhere. On the short-wave or high-frequency (HF) bands they could be coming from locations in the same country, or they may be from the other side of the globe. On the VHF and UHF bands the distances the signals have travelled are likely to be much shorter, but even so the transmissions can be just as interesting.

## THE LEGAL POSITION
Before we look at the transmissions that can be heard, it has to be mentioned that there are laws governing which ones are legal to receive. In the UK, the general rule is that it is legal to listen to transmissions that are transmitted for general reception. This includes broadcast transmissions (although a licence is required for television), standard frequency transmissions, radio amateurs and Citizens' Band (CB). It is *not* within the law to receive police messages, ship-to-shore transmissions, mobile telephone conversations and the like, where reception is intended by a specific person. Further information and

clarification can be found using the Ofcom information sheet *RA169* detailed in the 'Further Reading' note at the end of this chapter.

## TYPES OF TRANSMISSION
The actual type of transmission depends to a certain extent on the frequencies being monitored. The short-wave bands naturally tend to carry a large amount of long-haul traffic. International broadcasting is one obvious type of transmission. Radio amateurs also make use of their allocations in these bands. Many seek contacts world-wide, although on other bands more local contacts can be made. Citizens Band transmissions may also be heard.

Apart from these there are many other signals around. News agencies often send out information, and some of these are general broadcast transmissions intended for

*Image courtesy of Icom UK*

**A small handheld scanner.**

reception by anyone. There are also many ship-to-shore transmissions. Again, special bands are set aside for these. However, with the growing number of ships equipped with satellite communications, the level of traffic on the short-wave bands is decreasing.

There are also many other types of transmission. Some may be from embassies, some are military, some are general mobile transmissions, and there is a wide variety of other transmissions for different purposes and using different types of emission.

On the VHF and UHF bands there is the same variety of transmissions, but they are generally over a much shorter range. The most widely heard stations are VHF FM broadcasts that are found around 100MHz, and also UHF television transmissions. However, there are also radiotelephone systems, cellular telephones and many other point-to-point communications to be found on these frequencies. Aircraft use the frequencies just above the VHF / FM broadcast band. These transmissions include those between the aircraft and the control tower, and also many other short-range transmissions by people at the airport.

Apart from these there are many satellite signals. Meteorological satellites, communications satellites and also many communications occur for the manned space flights on these frequencies.

Radio amateurs also have

Aircraft make widespread use of radio.

| Freq (MHz) | | Band |
|---|---|---|
| 0.150 | - 0.285 | Long Wave |
| 0.5265 | - 1.6065 | Medium Wave |
| 2.300 | - 2.495 | 120 metres* |
| 3.200 | - 3.400 | 90 metres* |
| 3.900 | - 4.000 | 75 metres+ |
| 4.750 | - 5060 | 60 metres* |
| 5.900 | - 6.200 | 49 metres |
| 7.100 | - 7.350 | 41 metres** |
| 9.400 | - 9.900 | 31 metres |
| 11.600 | - 12.100 | 25 metres |
| 13.570 | - 13.870 | 22 metres |
| 15.100 | - 15.800 | 19 metres |
| 17.480 | - 17.900 | 16 metres |
| 18.900 | - 19.020 | 15 metres++ |
| 21.450 | - 21.850 | 13 metres |
| 25.600 | - 26.100 | 11 metres++ |

**Notes:**
\* 'Tropical band' for use in tropical areas only
+ Only allocated for broadcasting in Europe and Asia
\*\* The 41 metre broadcast band will relinquish the section 7.100 to 7.200MHz to the amateur service.
++ The 15 and 11 metre broadcast bands are seldom used at present.

**Table 3.1. Broadcast bands.**

allocations in this portion of the spectrum and they make good use of these frequencies.

## BROADCAST BANDS

One interesting aspect of short-wave listening is scanning the broadcast bands. By tuning around these bands it is possible to hear an enormous variety of stations, far more than those audible on the medium-wave band after dark. These broadcast in many languages, and it is possible to hear a good number broadcasting in English. Not only is it possible to hear news from other countries, and from another point of view, but many stations broadcast interesting programmes about their own countries.

There are many different bands on which these stations can be heard. The long-wave band generally carries very high-power stations that cover large areas. In the UK the BBC long-wave transmitter on 198kHz covers most of the UK, and there are many other equivalent stations within the areas of the world where the long-wave band is permitted as a broadcast band.

The medium-wave band is used for more regionalised broadcasting. Typically high-power stations may have a coverage area with a radius of a hundred miles or so. There are even a few international broadcast stations: the BBC World Service broadcasts from south-east England on 648kHz and other countries also have international medium-wave stations.

The bands higher in frequency are used for true international broadcasting. Of these, the 49-metre band is one of the busiest, with stations audible both day and night.

A short-wave broadcast station's curtain transmitting antenna.

Those at the high frequency end of the short-wave spectrum have less reliable propagation and stations may only be audible during the day and around the peak of the sunspot cycle. However, during these times stations are likely to be audible from all over the world.

The VHF / FM band is also interesting. Although stations are normally only audible over distances of a hundred kilometres or so, when there is a 'lift' in conditions due to tropospheric or Sporadic E propagation, stations much further afield may be heard.

## CITIZENS' BAND

Citizens' Band or CB radio is available in many countries, including the UK. The band that is almost universally used is to be found around 27MHz and operation is based around distinct channels. Dependent upon the country, operation is either freely available without the use of a licence, or a licence may be obtained with the minimum of formality. In the UK operation is on FM, while some other countries also allow the use of AM and SSB.

The idea of CB is very popular. Many people use it because it is a way of keeping in touch with friends from home or whilst on the move. Equipment is also reasonably cheap and easy to install, making it an ideal option for many people.

However, CB does not offer nearly as much as amateur radio. For example, there are far fewer bands, it is not possible to build your own equipment and distances are restricted. However, many people have entered amateur radio from CB and it can provide an introduction to radio. It is quite interesting to listen to CB transmissions, if nothing else to gain a feel for the hobby.

## AMATEUR RADIO

Throughout the radio spectrum there are frequency bands allocated to radio amateurs. Some are shared with other services but many are allocated only for the use of radio amateurs, such is the importance given to the hobby by the international community.

The lowest frequency band is found in the low-frequency portion of the spectrum, between 135.7 and 137.8kHz. The highest allocated to amateur radio is in the region of 250GHz, showing the vast range of frequencies available. It must be admitted that there is very little operation on the highest frequencies, because they represent a significant technical challenge. Fortunately there are plenty of stations on many of the other bands, especially those in the short-wave portion of the spectrum, and those in the VHF and UHF areas. It is always possible to hear stations, particularly on the short-wave bands, and even on the VHF and UHF bands (where ranges are shorter) there are large amounts of activity, especially at times when people are on the move and using equipment in their cars, or in the evenings and at weekends.

Listening to radio amateurs can be an interesting hobby in its own right. An enormous variety of different signals can be heard. On some bands signals can be heard over distances of many thousands of miles, whereas on others different and interesting types of communication may be used. Sound, television and data are all transmitted and can be received when the correct equipment is used. This wide variety is one of the factors that makes the hobby so interesting.

| Frequencies in MHz |
|---|
| 0.1357 - 0.1378 |
| 1.810  -  2.000 |
| 3.500  -  3.800 |
| 7.000  -  7.200 |
| 10.100 - 10.150 |
| 14.000 - 14.350 |
| 18.068 - 18.168 |
| 21.000 - 21.450 |
| 24.890 - 24.990 |
| 28.000 - 29.700 |
| 50.00  -  52.00 |
| 70.00  -  70.50 |
| 144.0  -  146.0 |
| 430.0  -  440.0 |
| 1240   -  1325 |
| 2310   -  2450 |
| 3400   -  3475 |
| 5650   -  5680 |
| 5755   -  5765 |
| 5820   -  5850 |
| 10,000 - 10,125 |

Table 3.2. UK amateur allocations below 10GHz.

**FURTHER INFORMATION**
*Amateur Radio Operating Manual*, 6th edn, Don Field, G3XTT, RSGB, 2005.
Ofcom advice on scanners etc is available on the Internet at:
http://www.ofcom.org.uk/radiocomms/ifi/enforcement/ofw156x

# 4. Jargon, Codes and Callsigns

ANYONE LISTENING to radio amateurs talk over the air will quickly discover that there are a lot of codes and jargon or terminology that are used. This has arisen out of the necessity to communicate quickly and effectively. In fact many of the codes were originally devised for use with Morse code. However, over the years they have been adopted for use in normal speech as well.

Fortunately it is not difficult to learn these codes and terms. They are very useful, and also help to break down any language barriers. Although English is used predominantly on the amateur bands, the use of these abbreviations and codes helps those people who do not speak the language so well to communicate quite effectively.

## ABBREVIATIONS

Many of the abbreviations shown in **Table 4.1** are quite obvious. Some are technical, for example 'AM' for amplitude modulation, while others like 'ABT' are contractions of words (in this case 'about'), and came about because of the need to send fewer letters to speed up Morse code transmissions. Not all of these are used in speech as they are not always applicable.

| | | | |
|---|---|---|---|
| ABT | about | LID | a poor operator |
| AGN | again | LW | long wire |
| AM | amplitude modulation | MOD | modulation |
| ANT | antenna | ND | nothing doing |
| BCI | broadcast interference | NW | now |
| BCNU | be seeing you | OB | old boy |
| BFO | beat frequency oscillator | OM | old man |
| BK | break | OP | operator |
| B4 | before | OT | old timer |
| CFM | confirm | PA | power amplifier |
| CLD | called | PSE | please |
| CIO | carrier insertion oscillator | R | roger (OK) |
| CONDX | conditions | RCVD | received |
| CPI | copy | RX | receiver |
| CQ | a general call | RTTY | radio teletype |
| CU | see you | SA | say |
| CUAGN | see you again | SED | said |
| CUD | could | SIGS | signals |
| CW | continuous wave or carrier wave (usually used to indicate a Morse code transmission) | SRI | sorry |
| | | SSB | single sideband |
| | | STN | station |
| DE | from | SWL | short wave listener |
| DX | long distance | TKS | thanks |
| ERE | here | TNX | thanks |
| ES | and | TU | thank you |
| FB | fine business | TVI | television interference |
| FER | for | TX | transmitter |
| FM | frequency modulation | U | you |
| FONE | telephony | UR | your, you are |
| GA | good afternoon | VY | very |
| GB | goodbye | WID | with |
| GD | good | WKD | worked |
| GE | good evening | WUD | would |
| GM | good morning | WX | weather |
| GN | goodnight | XMTR | transmitter |
| GND | ground | XTAL | crystal |
| HBREW | home brew (home made) | XYL | wife |
| HI | laughter | Z | GMT (the letter is added after the time, eg 1600Z) |
| HPE | hope | | |
| HR | here | YL | young lady |
| HV | have | 73 | best regards |
| HW | how | 88 | love and kisses |

**Table 4.1. Commonly used abbreviations.**

## MORSE CODE

The Morse code is probably the most famous of all the codes used for radio transmissions. It was originally devised in the middle of the 19th century by Samuel Morse for use with the old wire telegraph systems. With the introduction of radio it was found to be just as useful and it is still widely employed today because it has several advantages over other types of transmission, as described in the chapter on types of transmission. Although it is not a requirement to pass a Morse test now to gain an amateur radio licence in the UK, it is still useful to be able to send and receive Morse code as many amateur radio transmissions still use it.

| | | | | | |
|---|---|---|---|---|---|
| A | .‒ | N | ‒. | 1 | .‒‒‒‒ |
| B | ‒... | O | ‒‒‒ | 2 | ..‒‒‒ |
| C | ‒.‒. | P | .‒‒. | 3 | ...‒‒ |
| D | ‒.. | Q | ‒‒.‒ | 4 | ....‒ |
| E | . | R | .‒. | 5 | ..... |
| F | ..‒. | S | ... | 6 | ‒.... |
| G | ‒‒. | T | ‒ | 7 | ‒‒... |
| H | .... | U | ..‒ | 8 | ‒‒‒.. |
| I | .. | V | ...‒ | 9 | ‒‒‒‒. |
| J | .‒‒‒ | W | .‒‒ | 0 | ‒‒‒‒‒ |
| K | ‒.‒ | X | ‒..‒ | | |
| L | .‒.. | Y | ‒.‒‒ | | |
| M | ‒‒ | Z | ‒‒.. | | |

Table 4.2. The Morse code (letters and numerals).

| | | | |
|---|---|---|---|
| . (full stop) | .‒.‒.‒ | Start of work (CT) | ‒.‒.‒ |
| , (comma) | ‒‒..‒‒ | End of work (VA) | ...‒.‒ |
| ? (question mark) | ..‒‒.. | End of message (AR) | .‒.‒. |
| = (equals sign) | ‒...‒ | Invitation to transmit (K) | ‒.‒ |
| / (stroke) | ‒..‒. | Invitation to particular | |
| Mistake | ........ | station to transmit (KN) | ‒.‒‒. |

Table 4.3. The Morse code (punctuation and procedural characters. Note: Procedural characters made up of two letters are sent as a single letter with no break between them.

## PHONETIC ALPHABET

When spelling out place names or when giving callsigns it is necessary to ensure that the letters are understood precisely. It is very easy to confuse letters like 'B' and 'P' or 'S' and 'F', especially when talking over the radio and when interference levels are high. To stop this happening a *phonetic alphabet* is used. People will be heard giving their callsigns using this, for example "Golf three Yankee Whisky X-ray" for G3YWX. The one most commonly used and adopted internationally by the International Telecommunication Union is given in **Table 4.4**, although people will also be heard using different phonetics (such as "Germany" for 'G' rather than "Golf"; or "Mexico" for 'M' instead of "Mike").

| | | | |
|---|---|---|---|
| A | Alpha | N | November |
| B | Bravo | O | Oscar |
| C | Charlie | P | Papa |
| D | Delta | Q | Quebec |
| E | Echo | R | Romeo |
| F | Foxtrot | S | Sierra |
| G | Golf | T | Tango |
| H | Hotel | U | Uniform |
| I | India | V | Victor |
| J | Juliet | W | Whisky |
| K | Kilo | X | X-ray |
| L | Lima | Y | Yankee |
| M | Mike | Z | Zulu |

Table 4.4. The phonetic alphabet.

## RST CODE

When transmitting it is very useful to receive a signal report: it helps to guide how to conduct the contact. If strengths are low or interference levels are high, the contact can be kept short. Reports also help to determine how well the station is working. If reports are consistently poor it may indicate a problem with the station. To give meaningful reports it is necessary to have a consistent reporting system.

The system that is universally accepted for radio amateurs is known as the RST system. This consists of three figures, one each for readability, signal strength and tone. Their meanings are defined in **Table 4.5**. The final figure for tone is only used for Morse signals. For example a voice transmission that is readable with a little difficulty and is moderately strong would be given the report of "4 and 7". A Morse signal that is totally readable, strong, and has a pure DC note would be given a report of 589.

Many receivers incorporate signal strength, or 'S', meters and these can be helpful when trying to judge the strength of a station. The meters are calibrated in 'S' units up to S9 and then beyond that they are calibrated in decibels over S9. However, it should be remembered that S meters are notoriously inaccurate and should only be used as a guide.

**READABILITY**

| | |
|---|---|
| 1 | Unreadable |
| 2 | Barely readable |
| 3 | Readable with difficulty |
| 4 | Readable with little difficulty |
| 5 | Totally readable |

**STRENGTH**

| | |
|---|---|
| 1 | Faint, barely perceptible |
| 2 | Very weak |
| 3 | Weak |
| 4 | Fair |
| 5 | Fairly good |
| 6 | Good |
| 7 | Moderately strong |
| 8 | Strong |
| 9 | Very strong |

**TONE**

| | |
|---|---|
| 1 | Extremely rough note |
| 2 | Very rough note |
| 3 | Rough note |
| 4 | Fairly rough note |
| 5 | Note modulated with strong ripple |
| 6 | Modulated note |
| 7 | Near DC note but with smooth ripple |
| 8 | Good DC note with a trace of ripple |
| 9 | Pure DC note |

Table 4.5. The RST code for reporting signal reception.

## THE Q CODE

One of the commonly used codes is known as the Q code. It is used not only by radio amateurs but also by maritime and aeronautical stations. The complete code is very extensive and covers many aspects. Many of the codes are not of interest to radio amateurs but those that are of interest are listed in **Table 4.6** over the page.

The code is designed for use either as a question or as an answer. For example "QSL?" means "Do you acknowledge receipt?", whereas when used as an answer "QSL" means "I acknowledge receipt". In the table both the question and answer forms are given.

Often radio amateurs will be heard using these codes as part of ordinary speech because they are so convenient. For example, someone may be heard to say "the QRM is bad" when they mean that there is a high level of man-made interference; they may be "going QRT", meaning they are going to close down, or they may be heard talking about "QSL cards" - the cards used to confirm a contact.

| Q Code question | Meaning | Q Code answer | Meaning |
|---|---|---|---|
| QRA? | What is the name of your station? | QRA | The name of my station is . . . |
| QRG? | What is my frequency? | QRG | Your exact frequency is . . . |
| QRL? | Are you busy? | QRL | I am busy |
| QRM? | Is there any (man made) interference? | QRM | There is (man made) interference |
| QRN? | Is there any atmospheric noise? | QRN | There is atmospheric noise |
| QRO? | Shall I increase my power? | QRO | Increase power |
| QRP? | Shall I reduce power? | QRP | Reduce power |
| QRQ? | Shall I send faster? | QRQ | Send faster |
| QRS? | Shall I send more slowly? | QRS | Send more slowly |
| QRT? | Shall I stop sending? | QRT | Stop sending |
| QRU? | Do you have any messages for me? | QRU | I have nothing for you |
| QRV? | Are you ready to receive? | QRV | I am ready |
| QRZ? | Who is calling me? | QRZ | You are being called by . . . |
| QSL? | Can you acknowledge receipt? | QSL | I acknowledge receipt |
| QSP? | Can you relay a message? | QSP | I can relay a message |
| QSY? | Shall I change to another frequency? | QSY | Change to another frequency |
| QTH? | What is your location? | QTH | My location is . . . |
| QTR? | What is the exact time? | QTR | The exact time is . . . |

Table 4.6. The Q code.

## CALLSIGNS

Every licensed amateur radio transmitting station is issued with a callsign that it must use to identify itself over the air. It is possible to tell quite a bit about the station from its callsign; in particular to identify the country where it is located.

All callsigns have a similar format, consisting of two parts: a prefix and a suffix. The prefix normally consists of up to three characters up to and including the last numeral. Either it may consist of one or two letters followed by a number, or a number, letter and then a final number (eg GW8FEO, 2E1DBI). It is the prefix that enables the location of the station to be determined.

The remaining part of the callsign normally consists of up to three letters and these are the serial letters for the particular station. For example, in the callsign G3YWX, the prefix is G3 and the serial letters are YWX. In this instance the prefix shows the station is located in England. There is a growing number of exceptions to these rules. Usually they are special event stations, or DXpeditions to rare locations. An abbreviated list of prefixes is given in **Table 4.6** below and on the following pages. A full list is given in the *RSGB Prefix Guide*.

| | | | | | |
|---|---|---|---|---|---|
| A2 | Botswana | C5 | Gambia | DA - DR | Germany |
| A3 | Tonga | C6 | Bahamas | DS | South Korea |
| A4 | Oman | C9 | Mozambique | DU - DZ | Philippines |
| A5 | Bhutan | CE | Chile | E2 | Thailand |
| A6 | United Arab Emirates | CN | Morocco | E3 | Eritrea |
| A7 | Qatar | CO | Cuba | E4 | Palestine |
| A9 | Bahrain | CP | Bolivia | E5 | Cook Islands |
| AA - AL | USA (see K series for further details) | CT | Portugal | EA | Spain |
| | | CT3 | Madeira | EA6 | Balearic Is |
| AP | Pakistan | CU | Azores | EA8 | Canary Is |
| B | China | CX | Uruguay | EA9 | Ceuta and Melilla |
| BV | Taiwan | D2 | Angola | EI | Ireland |
| C2 | Nauru | D4 | Cape Verde | EK | Armenia |
| C3 | Andorra | D6 | Comoros | EL | Liberia |

| | | | | | |
|---|---|---|---|---|---|
| EP | Iran | JX | Jan Mayen | S2 | Bangladesh |
| ER | Moldova | JY | Jordan | S5 | Slovenia |
| ES | Estonia | K | USA, inc: | S7 | Seychelles |
| ET | Ethiopia | KG4xx | Guantanamo Bay | S9 | Sao Tome and Principe |
| EU - EW | Belarus | KH1 | Baker & Howland Is | SA - SM | Sweden |
| EX | Kyrgyzstan | KH2 | Guam | SN - SP | Poland |
| EY | Tajikistan | KH3 | Johnston I | ST | Sudan |
| EZ | Turkmenistan | KH4 | Midway I | SU | Egypt |
| F | France | KH5 | Palmyra & Jarvis Is | SV | Greece |
| FG | Guadeloupe | KH6, 7 | Hawaii | SV5 | Dodecanese Is |
| FH | Mayotte | KH8 | American Samoa | SV9 | Crete |
| FJ | St Barthelemy | KH9 | Wake I | T2 | Tuvalu |
| FK | New Caledonia | KH0 | Northern Mariana Is | T3 | Kiribati |
| FM | Martinique | KL | Alaska | T7 | San Marino |
| FO | French Polynesia | KP1 | Navassa I | T8 | Palau |
| FP | St Pierre & Miquelon | KP2 | US Virgin Is | T9 | Bosnia-Herzegovina |
| FR | Reunion I | KP3, 4 | Puerto Rico | TA | Turkey |
| FS | French St Martin | KP5 | Desecheo I | TF | Iceland |
| FW | Wallis and Futuna Is | LA | Norway | TG | Guatemala |
| FY | French Guiana | LU | Argentina | TI | Costa Rica |
| G | England | LX | Luxembourg | TJ | Cameroon |
| GB | UK Special Event Stns | LY | Lithuania | TK | Corsica |
| GD | Isle of Man | LZ | Bulgaria | TL | Central African Republic |
| GI | Northern Ireland | M | England | TN | Congo |
| GJ | Jersey | MD | Isle of Man | TR | Gabon |
| GM | Scotland | MI | Northern Ireland | TT | Chad |
| GU | Guernsey | MJ | Jersey | TU | Cote d'Ivoire |
| GW | Wales | MM | Scotland | TY | Benin |
| H4 | Solomon Is | MU | Guernsey | TZ | Mali |
| HA | Hungary | MW | Wales | UA - UI | Russia |
| HB | Switzerland | N | USA (see K series for | UA2 | Kaliningrad |
| HB0 | Liechtenstein | | further details) | UK | Uzbekistan |
| HC | Ecuador | OA | Peru | UN | Kazakhstan |
| HH | Haiti | OD | Lebanon | UR - UU | Ukraine |
| HI | Dominican Republic | OE | Austria | UX - UY | Ukraine |
| HK | Colombia | OH | Finland | V2 | Antigua & Barbuda |
| HL | Korea | OH0 | Åland Is | V3 | Belize |
| HP | Panama | OJ0 | Market Reef | V4 | St Kitts and Nevis |
| HR | Honduras | OK, OL | Czech Republic | V5 | Namibia |
| HS | Thailand | OM | Slovak Republic | V6 | Micronesia |
| HV | Vatican | ON - OT | Belgium | V7 | Marshall Is |
| HZ | Saudi Arabia | OX | Greenland | V8 | Brunei |
| I | Italy | OY | Faeroe Is | VA - VG | Canada |
| IS0 | Sardinia | OZ | Denmark | VK | Australia |
| J2 | Djibouti | P2 | Papua New Guinea | VO, VY | Canada |
| J3 | Grenada | P4 | Aruba | VP2E | Anguilla |
| J5 | Guinea-Bissau | P5 | North Korea | VP2M | Montserrat |
| J6 | St Lucia | PA - PI | Netherlands | VP2V | British Virgin Is |
| J7 | Dominica | PJ | Netherlands West Indies | VP5 | Turks and Caicos Is |
| J8 | St Vincent & Grenadines | PY | Brazil | VP6 | Pitcairn Is |
| JA - JS | Japan | PZ | Suriname | VP8 | Falkland Is, South |
| JT | Mongolia | R | Russia | | Georgia, Antarctica |
| JW | Svalbard | S0 | Western Sahara | VP9 | Bermuda |

| | | | | | |
|---|---|---|---|---|---|
| VQ9 | Chagos Is | ZK2 | Niue | 5N | Nigeria |
| VR2 | Hong Kong | ZK3 | Tokelau Is | 5P - 5Q | Denmark |
| VU | India | ZL | New Zealand | 5R | Madagascar |
| W | USA (see K series for further details) | ZP | Paraguay | 5T | Mauritania |
| | | ZS | South Africa | 5U | Niger |
| XE | Mexico | 2D | Isle of Man | 5V | Togo |
| XT | Burkina | 2E | England | 5W | Samoa |
| XU | Cambodia | 2I | Northern Ireland | 5X | Uganda |
| XV | Vietnam | 2J | Jersey | 5Z | Kenya |
| XW | Laos | 2M | Scotland | 6O | Somalia |
| XX9 | Macau | 2U | Guernsey | 6V, 6W | Senegal |
| XY, XZ | Myanmar | 2W | Wales | 6Y | Jamaica |
| YA | Afghanistan | 3A | Monaco | 7J - 7N | Japan |
| YB - YF | Indonesia | 3B6, 7 | St Brandon & Agalega | 7O | Yemen |
| YI | Iraq | 3B8 | Mauritius | 7P | Lesotho |
| YJ | Vanuatu | 3B9 | Rodrigues I | 7Q | Malawi |
| YK | Syria | 3C | Equatorial Guinea | 7X | Algeria |
| YL | Latvia | 3D2 | Fiji | 8P | Barbados |
| YN | Nicaragua | 3DA0 | Swaziland | 8Q | Maldives |
| YO | Romania | 3V | Tunisia | 8R | Guyana |
| YS | El Salvador | 3W | Vietnam | 9A | Croatia |
| YT, YU | Serbia | 3X | Guinea | 9G | Ghana |
| YV | Venezuela | 4J, 4K | Azerbaijan | 9H | Malta |
| Z2 | Zimbabwe | 4L | Georgia | 9J | Zambia |
| Z3 | Macedonia | 4O | Montenegro | 9K | Kuwait |
| ZA | Albania | 4S | Sri Lanka | 9L | Sierra Leone |
| ZB | Gibraltar | 4U1ITU | ITU HQ, Geneva | 9M | Malaysia |
| ZC | UK Sovereign Bases on Cyprus | 4U1UN | UN HQ, New York | 9N | Nepal |
| | | 4W | East Timor | 9Q | Dem Rep of Congo |
| ZD7 | St Helena | 4X, 4Z | Israel | 9U | Burundi |
| ZD8 | Ascension I | 5A | Libya | 9V | Singapore |
| ZD9 | Tristan da Cunha | 5B | Cyprus | 9X | Rwanda |
| ZF | Cayman Is | 5H | Tanzania | 9Y | Trinidad and Tobago |

**Table 4.6. Abbreviated callsign prefix list. A full list is given in the *RSGB Prefix Guide*.**

## CALL AREAS

Some countries are split into *call areas* or *call districts*, where different prefixes are allocated according to the area of the country in which the station is located.

An example of this is the USA, where the number in the prefix changes according to the call area as shown in **Fig 4.1**. Stations in California have the number 6 in the callsign, eg W6, K6 etc. Those in the New England states have the figure 1, eg W1, K1 etc. It should be noted that the call areas for the USA refer to the area where the call was *issued*.

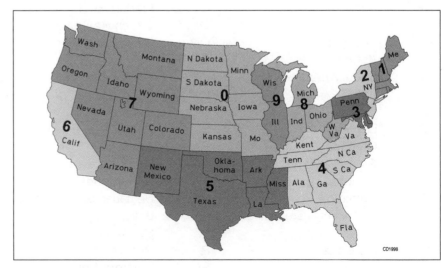

Fig 4.1. USA call areas.

If the licensee moves state he will not necessarily change his callsign, so some stations may be in different states to those inferred by the call number.

Occasionally additional letters may be added to the callsign. If a station is mobile, ie in a vehicle, it is normal to add the suffix '/M', and similarly for maritime mobile the letters '/MM' are used. Occasionally aeronautical mobile stations may be heard operating from an aircraft, and they use the suffix '/AM'. The suffix '/P' is used for portable stations. Other suffixes may also be heard from time to time.

With international travel being far more common these days, stations are often able to operate in other countries. When stations operate like this they generally use their home callsign with the prefix of the relevant country placed in front of it. For example, W6/G3YWX would be used by an English station operating from California. Occasionally the home callsign may be used with the prefix of the country in which the station is located added *after* the callsign as a suffix. However, this practice is less common these days.

**FURTHER INFORMATION**
*RSGB Prefix List*, Fred Handscombe, G4BWP (ed), (updated frequently), RSGB.
*RSGB Yearbook*, Steve White, G3ZVW (ed), RSGB.

# 5. Radio Propagation

THE WAY IN which radio signals travel, or *propagate*, is a particularly interesting topic. In some cases signals may only be heard over distances of a few miles, whereas under other circumstances signals from the other side of the world may be audible. Understanding how to use radio propagation conditions to their best is a skill that can be learned. Knowing when to listen and what frequencies to use can mean the difference between frequently being able to hear or contact stations from far afield, or just making the occasional long-distance contact. Those interested in making long-distance contacts spend time delving into the fascinating topic of radio propagation and using the conditions to their best. Even for those not interested in such contacts, a good knowledge of the topic can be interesting and beneficial.

## RADIO WAVES

Radio waves are basically the same as light or ultra-violet waves. The difference is that the wavelength (and hence the frequency) are different. Fortunately it is not necessary to have an in-depth knowledge of them, but there are a few useful aspects worth understanding. In terms of theory it is more than sufficient to know that they consist of two components, namely an electric component and a magnetic component.

To gain a very basic idea of the way in which radio waves travel, a signal can be likened to a stone being dropped into a pond where the ripples spread out in all directions away from the centre point where the stone entered the water. As they spread out the waves reduce in height (amplitude), but cover a larger area. The same is true of radio waves where they become weaker as distances increase from the transmitter.

There are several points that can be noted about the waves. The first is that they have a distinct *wavelength*. This is the distance between a point on one wave and the same point on the next one. Normally the most convenient point to note is the crest or peak of the wave.

The wavelengths of radio waves are normally measured in metres. They vary over a wide range and may be many thousands of metres long, or they may be as short as a few millimetres. In years past the position of a station on the radio dial was measured in metres, and we still talk about the 'long-wave' broadcast band, the 'medium-wave' band and the 'short-wave' bands.

Another point that can be seen about the waves is that they vibrate at a certain frequency. Returning to the pond analogy, if the ripples pass a certain point in the pond, eg a stick in the water, then the water surface will be seen to go up and down several times as the waves pass. The rate at which the level 'vibrates' is known as the *frequency*. This is measured in *hertz*, ie the number of cycles per second. These days the frequency of a signal is normally used to determine its position on a radio dial. Radio frequency signals are measured in many thousands, millions or even thousands of millions of hertz. Therefore frequencies measured in kilohertz (thousands of hertz), megahertz (millions of hertz), and gigahertz (thousand millions of hertz) are often seen.

As might be imagined there is a relationship between the frequency and wavelength. The longer the wavelength, the lower the frequency. They are linked by the velocity of the wave. For radio waves (and other electromagnetic waves) this is the speed of light. For most applications this can be taken to be 300,000,000 metres per second. If either the frequency or the wavelength is known, it is very easy to work out the other. There is a simple formula where multiplying the frequency and wavelength equals the speed of light:

$$\lambda \times f = c$$

- where $\lambda$ (lambda) is the wavelength in metres (m); f is the frequency in hertz (Hz); and c is the speed of light (300,000,000 metres per second).

Take as an example a station broadcasting in the medium-wave band that has a signal on a frequency of 1 megahertz (1MHz). By inserting the right figures into the formula it can be seen that it has a wavelength of 300m.

## THE RADIO SPECTRUM

Radio signals exist over a vast range of frequencies. At the low end of the range transmissions exist on frequencies below 50kHz. At the other end of the spectrum transistors and other devices are being developed that operate at frequencies in excess of 100GHz. In order to clarify the radio spectrum it is split up into different areas as shown in **Fig 5.1**.

Within these areas are contained all the familiar transmissions we hear each day. The medium-wave broadcast band is contained within the MF portion of the spectrum. The short-wave bands are located in the HF area. The VHF area contains a wide variety of transmissions including the VHF / FM broadcast band and many point-to-point and mobile communications. At UHF we find the analogue television transmissions, mobile phones and much more.

Within these areas there are many bands allocated to amateur radio. As they are spread over such a wide frequency range, this means that there is an enormous variation in the characteristics they offer. Some are able to support world-wide communications with reflections from the ionosphere, whilst others are used for local transmissions, and other frequencies are able to support communications via satellites. The way in which radio signals travel on different frequencies means that some bands are able to support one type of transmission better than others, giving each band its own 'feel'. Selecting the best band for a given purpose means it is possible to make the best use of it.

## RADIO PROPAGATION

The way in which radio waves travel around the world is dependent upon a number of things. In free space signals travel in straight lines, but when signals are transmitted around the earth, they are influenced by several factors. The first is obviously the earth itself. The areas of the atmosphere also have a major effect, different areas affecting different frequencies.

## GROUND WAVE

Signals like those on the long- and medium-wave bands propagate primarily as *ground waves*. As the name suggests, here the signal spreads out away from the transmitter along the ground, as shown in **Fig 5.2**. It might normally be expected that it would only be heard over a distance equal to the line of sight, because radio waves are basically the same as light. However, signals can be heard over much greater distances than this. High-power medium-wave stations can typically be heard over distances of 150km and more. The reason for this is that the signal interacts with the earth and this slows that part of the wave closest to it. This results in the wave front being angled towards the earth so that it can follow its curvature.

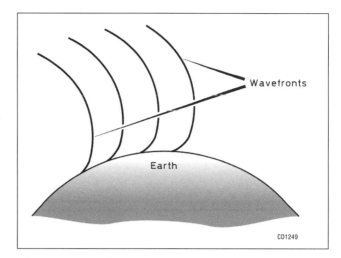

Fig 5.2. Ground wave.

## THE ATMOSPHERE

Before looking at the way in which signals propagate through the earth's atmosphere it is necessary to take a brief look at it to discover something about its make-up. The atmosphere can be seen as a number of areas stretching from ground level right up to altitudes in excess of 500km, as shown in **Fig 5.3**. Within some of these areas the radio signals can be bent and reflected so that they return to ground many miles away from where they were transmitted. Some areas have a significant effect, whilst others have very little or none. The two main areas that affect radio signals are the ionosphere and the troposphere. Each acts on signals in a different way, and broadly affect different areas of the radio spectrum.

## THE IONOSPHERE

It is the ionosphere that is responsible for world-wide communications on the short-wave bands. It is an area in the upper atmosphere where there are relatively high levels of ionisation.

This is caused because radiation from the sun is so strong that when it strikes the gas molecules electrons are released, leaving ions. Whilst it is the ions that give their name to the ionosphere it is actually the electrons that affect the radio waves.

The ionosphere is often considered as a number of layers. In actual fact, they are just various areas where the

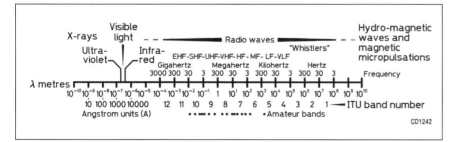

Fig 5.1. The radio spectrum.

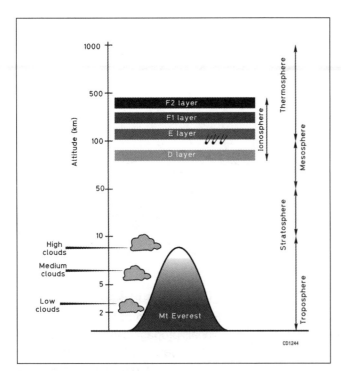

Fig 5.3. The atmosphere.

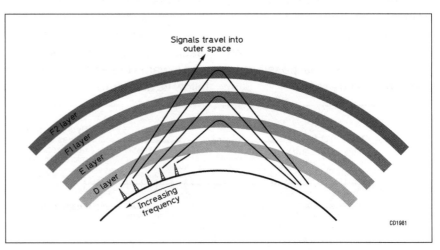

Fig 5.4. The layers of the ionosphere over the course of a day.

levels of electrons reach a peak, but nevertheless it is a convenient way to look at it. There are three main layers in the ionosphere. These are imaginatively termed the 'D', 'E', and 'F' layers (see **Fig 5.3**). The D layer is only present during the day and disappears after dark. It absorbs signals that are low in frequency. The results of this can be seen by the fact that medium-wave broadcast stations are only heard over relatively short distances during the day. At night when the layer disappears signals are able to reach the higher, reflecting layers and stations can be heard from much further afield.

The next layer up is known as the E layer. Like the D layer this is only present during the day, although a small amount of residual ionisation may remain overnight. This layer serves to reflect (or, more correctly, refract) radio signals. The degree to which this happens may be sufficient to reflect them back to the earth.

Above the E layer there is a further layer known as the F layer. During the day this often splits into two layers, known as F1 and F2, as shown in **Fig 5.4**. At night when it is

not exposed to the sun's radiation, the level of ionisation falls and it normally forms a single layer. It is the F layer that is responsible for most of the very long-distance communications on the short-wave bands. Like the E layer it also reflects radio signals.

## REFLECTION BY THE IONOSPHERE

The way in which the ionosphere affects radio signals varies with their frequency. To illustrate how this happens take the example where a

low-frequency signal is first transmitted. This might be a signal in the medium-wave band. During the day a ground wave will spread out from the transmitting antenna. Some of the signal will also be transmitted upwards. This is known as the sky wave. However, as the D layer will be present during the day the sky wave is absorbed.

If the frequency is increased, the signal will start to penetrate the D layer and it will reach the E layer, as shown in **Fig 5.5**. Here the signal will be refracted so that it can be returned to earth where it will be heard at some distance away from the transmitter.

Fig 5.5. Propagation using the ionosphere at different frequencies.

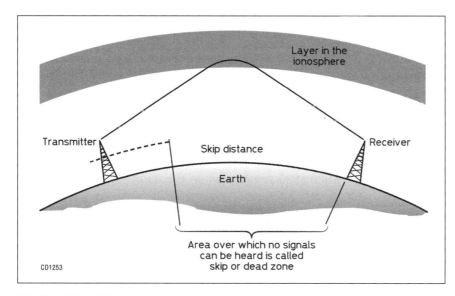

Fig 5.6. Skip distance.

This will normally be further away than where the ground wave can extend, and so the distances reached are increased.

If the frequency is increased still further, the signal will start to penetrate the E layer and it will eventually pass straight through it, travelling onwards until it reaches the F1 layer. Here again it will be refracted back to earth, but then as the frequency is increased still further it will pass on to the F2 layer, being refracted back to earth.

Ultimately a frequency will be reached where the signal will pass through all the layers so that it travels on into outer space.

The other effect that is noticed is that as the frequency of the signal is increased the distance over which propagation by ground wave occurs decreases. This is one reason why short-wave broadcast stations are heard via the ground wave over short distances when compared with medium-wave stations, despite the fact that very high powers might be used.

## SKIP DISTANCE
When a signal reaches the ionosphere and is refracted back to earth it will be heard over a wide area because the angle at which the signal reaches the ionosphere is quite wide.

Even so, there is normally a zone where the signal can not be heard. This occurs in the area beyond the ground wave but before the sky wave returns to earth. This is known as the skip zone, and the distance from the transmitter to where the signal is heard is known as the skip distance (see **Fig 5.6**).

## VARIATIONS IN THE IONOSPHERE
The state of the ionosphere is constantly changing. The time of day, season and the state of the sun all play their part. At night when the ionosphere does not receive radiation from the sun, the D layer disappears, the E layer nearly disappears and the level of ionisation in the F layer falls. The seasons also have an effect. In just the same way that the earth receives less sunshine in winter, so the ionosphere receives less radiation.

The state of the sun also has a major effect. The level of the types of radiation that cause ionisation is dependent upon the number of sunspots (see photo, right). These vary in number very roughly in line with a cycle that is about 11 years in length. Other changes on the sun, such as solar flares, can cause radio conditions to change drastically, giving problems with reception of short-wave transmissions.

With all these variations, predicting the state of the ionosphere can be a bit like predicting the weather. However, after some listening on the bands it is possible to get a feel for the general pattern of radio conditions with the changes in time of day and the season.

The descriptions of some of the amateur bands in a later chapter give a more detailed view of the conditions that are likely to be expected. However, it is possible to give a very brief overview. Signals below about 2MHz travel primarily by ground wave during the day. At night, as the D layer disappears signals much further afield can be heard with distances of 2000km not being uncommon.

Signals above 2MHz and below about 10MHz can often be heard over distances of a few hundred to possibly 2000km during the day. At night distances again increase, and on some frequencies distances of 3000km may easily be achieved.

Above 10MHz the balance starts to change. Long-distance communications are also possible during the day, and those bands particularly at the high-frequency end of the shortwave spectrum may only support communication via the ionosphere during the day. On these bands signals may often be heard at remarkable strengths from great distances, even the other side of the globe. At these frequencies the effect of the season and the sunspot cycle have a marked effect. At the trough

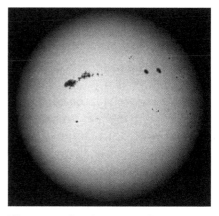

The sun, showing several sunspots.

of the sunspot cycle ionospheric communications may only be possible on frequencies up to 20MHz or a little more. At the peak, frequencies of 50MHz and more may be used.

## TROPOSPHERIC PROPAGATION

The ionosphere is not the only region of the atmosphere that affects radio waves. The troposphere can also change the path over which they travel. The density of the air and the amount of water vapour that it contains change the refractive index of the air. As a result the index increases slightly towards the ground. Light bends towards an area of higher refractive index, and this can be demonstrated by putting a stick into water and seeing the way in which the stick appears to be bent. Radio waves, particularly those above 30MHz, act in the same way, and under normal conditions it is found that the range of a VHF transmitter may be extended by at least a third beyond the horizon.

Tropospheric propagation of this nature primarily affects the VHF and UHF bands. It is not particularly apparent on the short-wave bands, even when there is no propagation via the ionosphere.

Under certain conditions the change in refractive index of the air can be much greater and the degree of bending of radio signals is accordingly much higher. This enables signals to be heard over much greater distances. Sometimes they may even be trapped in a duct. When this happens, VHF / UHF signals may be heard over distances of possibly 1500km.

When the propagation conditions are improved, talk may be heard on the bands of a 'lift'. These improvements can be brought about in a number of ways. When an area of high atmospheric pressure is present there is a good likelihood of improved radio conditions.

## OTHER MODES

There are many other modes of propagation that are available to the short-wave listener and radio amateur. These normally tend to be comparatively short-lived and often occur only when a particular set of conditions is present.

*Sporadic E (E$_s$)* is one such case. This occurs when small areas in the E layer become very highly ionised. The reason for this is not fully understood and occurrences of it cannot be predicted. In temperate zones like the UK it occurs more frequently in summer. The level of ionisation is very high and frequencies as high as 150MHz can be refracted back to earth, although these openings may be very short, often only a few minutes. When Sporadic E occurs the frequencies that are affected slowly rise, affecting amateur bands like 28MHz first, and higher frequencies later as the ionisation builds up. Having reached a peak, the level of ionisation falls slowly away. In periods of low sunspot activity Sporadic E gives useful openings on the 28MHz band, and communications are often possible on the 50MHz band as well. It is also found that the geographical areas that are affected change during the course of an opening. The reason for this is that the area or 'cloud' of ionisation is blown about by the winds in the upper atmosphere.

Another type of propagation used on the VHF bands is known as *meteor scatter* (**Fig 5.7**). This requires high power transmitters, sensitive receivers and effective antenna systems. All through the day the earth's atmosphere is bombarded by small meteors. At certain times of the year meteor showers are experienced when the number of meteors rises very considerably. As the meteors enter the earth's atmosphere they burn up, leaving a trail of ionisation behind them. This is sufficiently highly ionised to reflect radio signals up to frequencies of 150MHz and more. Although the ionisation only lasts for a very short time, possibly a second or so, this is sufficient to send some high-speed data, often in the form of very high-speed Morse code. In view of the unusual nature of this form of propagation very specialised operating techniques are also required.

Another form of propagation that can be used on the VHF bands occurs when an *aurora* is present. Flares from the sun throw out enormous quantities of material. When this reaches the earth it can cause visible auroras to occur. These are known as the northern (or southern) lights and are spectacular to see.

There is also an effect on radio signals. The normal ionospheric propagation can be disturbed on the

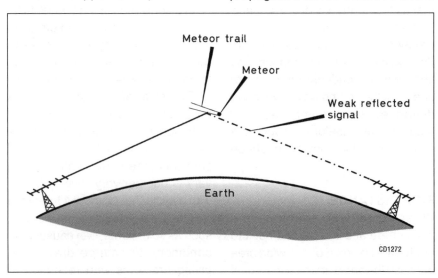

**Fig 5.7. Meteor scatter propagation.**

An aurora (northern lights) can reflect VHF radio signals.

to the earth.

Using these satellites can be very interesting. It demonstrates yet another area where radio amateurs are using the latest technology in their hobby.

short-wave bands but there are areas of intense ionisation extending from the earth's polar regions. By aiming the signals towards the areas of ionisation, they can be reflected back and heard over considerable distances. Signals that have been reflected in this way have a very distinctive 'rasping' tone because of the continually mobile nature of the ionisation. Not all stations are able to take advantage of this type of propagation: it is dependent on the size of the auroral 'event' and how far the ionisation extends outwards from the poles. Often stations in Scotland will be able to take advantage of a smaller aurora, whereas stations in southern England may not.

Another interesting mode of propagation is known as **moonbounce**. As the name implies, this type of propagation entails bouncing a signal off the surface of the moon. In view of the enormous distances involved and the small amount of signal reflected back to earth, very high powers, very sensitive receivers, and high-gain antennas are all required. Many people use large 'dish' antennas to achieve the required results. Despite the many difficulties of this mode of propagation, contacts can be made over enormous distances on the higher VHF frequencies and above.

## SATELLITES

Yet another way of transmitting signals over great distances is to use an artificial satellite. This technology is widely used by commercial users and whilst it may seem too expensive for amateur radio organisations to consider, there are in fact several amateur satellites in use. In general these use bands in the VHF and UHF regions, transmitting on one band and receiving on another.

Most of the satellites are in what is termed a low-earth orbit (LEO). This means that the satellites move around the earth unlike the much higher geostationary orbit where they remain in the same position relative

**FURTHER INFORMATION**
*Radio Propagation - Principles and Practice*, Ian Poole, G3YWX, RSGB, 2004.
*Radio Communication Handbook*, 8th edn, Mike Dennison, G3XDV, and Chris Lorek, G4HCL (eds), RSGB, 2005.

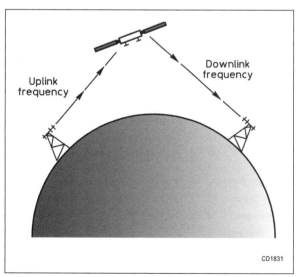

Fig 5.8. Communications using a satellite.

# 6. Bands and Band Plans

AMATEUR RADIO allocations or bands are present in most areas of the radio spectrum. Each band has its own characteristics, resulting from a number of factors. These include the propagation, other users who may share the band, the equipment available, and several other factors. This means that for a particular type of contact one band may be better than another. Knowing what the bands are like and when best to use them is one of the operating skills that will quickly be learned. Knowing where to look for particular types of transmission is also vital.

In order to make the best use of the available spectrum, *band plans* have been introduced. These give a guide to the types of transmission that can be used in the different areas of the band. This helps to reduce the levels of interference and makes the most efficient use of the spectrum.

The following are examples taken from the band plans that were valid for use in the UK when they were issued in 2006.

### 135.7 - 137.8kHz

This band is the lowest frequency amateur allocation and has only become available for radio amateurs in the past few years. With more countries releasing the band for amateur use the level of activity is beginning to rise.

In view of its place at the very low end of the frequency spectrum, it presents a unique challenge both in terms of operating and the technology that is used. Morse is generally used because it occupies very little bandwidth; several tens of Morse transmissions can be accommodated in this small band, whereas it is only wide enough for a single voice transmission. Many people use *very* slow Morse combined with exceedingly narrow filter bandwidths and digital signal processing techniques. Full-sized antennas for these frequencies would be very large so people use much smaller antennas. This presents new challenges for amateurs who use these frequencies.

While activity levels are still low when compared with the more popular bands, interest is growing and operating on these frequencies is particularly rewarding. There is no specific band plan for this band.

### 1.81 - 2.00MHz (160m) ('TOPBAND')

This band is often used for relatively local communications. Being just above the medium-wave broadcast band it possesses very similar characteristics. During the day distances of up to about 50km are possible, dependent upon the antennas in use. However, after dark when the D layer disappears the distances that can be achieved increase considerably, and stations from distances of over 1000km are often heard. It is possible for transatlantic contacts to be made, and at times it is even possible for stations at the other side of the globe to appear.

A challenge is to radiate a good signal from a small garden as a full-size antenna can be 80m long. The atmospheric noise levels are relatively high and this can make listening more difficult at times, but nevertheless gives the band its distinctive character.

The allocations for this band vary slightly from one country to the next. Many have full access to frequencies between 1.8 and 2.00MHz but some have restricted allocations. The band plan for the UK is given in **Table 6.1**. NB: Narrow-band modes include

| UK Band Plan Frequencies (MHz) | | Usage |
|---|---|---|
| 1.810 - 1.838 | | Morse only |
| 1.838 - 1.840 | | Narrow-band modes |
| 1.840 - 1.843 | | All modes |
| 1.843 - 2.000 | | Telephony and Morse |
| | 1.836 | QRP |
| | 1.960 | Direction Finding Contest beacons |

Table 6.1. 160 metres ('Topband') (1.81 - 2.00MHz).

Morse and many digital modes or 'digimodes', eg packet radio, AmTOR, etc, that occupy only a narrow bandwidth.

### 3.50 - 3.80MHz (80m)

80m is a very popular band for local contacts. During the daytime contacts up to distances of 200 or 300km can be made relatively easily.

After dark, distances increase with the disappearance of the D layer. It is quite easy for stations at distances around 1500km to be heard, and stations from the other side of the Atlantic can frequently be heard. Transmissions from the other side of the globe can be received, especially around dusk and dawn during spring and autumn.

Interference levels can be high. Atmospheric noise is not as high as that on 'topband', but interference from other stations is higher because the band is shared by other services.

Nevertheless the band is popular and worth using as it can be very handy for short-haul contacts whilst still being able to provide the ability to hear or contact long-distance stations.

| UK Band Plan Frequencies (MHz) | | Usage |
|---|---|---|
| 7.000 - 7.035 | | Morse only |
| | 7.030 | QRP centre of activity |
| 7.035 - 7.040 | | Narrow-band modes |
| | 7.038 - 7.040 | Narrow-band modes - automatically controlled data stations (unattended) |
| 7.040 – 7.043 | | All modes - automatically controlled data stations (unattended) |
| | 7.043 | Image modes centre of activity |
| 7.043 - 7.100 | | All modes excluding digimodes |
| | 7.045 | May be used for UK emergency traffic. |
| | 7.060 | IARU Region 1 centre of activity for emergency traffic |
| 7.100 - 7.200 | | No band plan at present |

Table 6.3. 40 metres (7.0 - 7.2MHz).

In Europe the allocation of 80m only extends to 3.8MHz. In North America the allocation extends to 4.0MHz. The UK 80m band plan is shown in **Table 6.2**.

### 7.00 - 7.20MHz (40m)

Although narrow, the 40m band is a very good hunting ground for people wanting to chase long-distance stations. During the day distances of 1000 to 2000km can be achieved but after dark these distances rise significantly. Transatlantic contacts are fairly common and stations from all over the globe may be heard at different times.

Naturally the seasons affect the propagation conditions. In the summer it is usually necessary to wait until nightfall for long-distance stations to appear, although in the winter they may often be heard at almost any time.

Again the allocation available in North America is greater than in Europe, as it extends to 7.3MHz. This can make it difficult for those in Europe to hear North American phone stations because the frequencies between 7.1 and 7.3MHz are used by broadcast stations in Europe. In recent years the portion of the band between 7.1 and 7.2 MHz has been re-assigned for amateur use. It is currently available in some European countries, including the UK, on a non-interference basis, and the deadline for the broadcast stations that currently use it to vacate the band is 2009. The UK 40m band plan is shown in **Table 6.3**.

### 10.100 - 10.150MHz (30m)

This band was released after a World Administrative Radio Conference (WARC) held in 1979. It is allocated to radio amateurs on a secondary basis with other services having preference. Accordingly it has been agreed that only narrow-band modes

| UK Band Plan Frequencies (MHz) | | Usage |
|---|---|---|
| 3.500 - 3.580 | | Morse |
| | 3.500 - 3.510 | Priority for inter-continental contacts |
| | 3.510 - 3.560 | Preferred section for contest contacts (3.555 slow telegraphy centre of activity) |
| | 3.560 - 3.580 | QRP (3.560 QRP centre of activity) |
| 3.580 - 3.600 | | Narrow-band modes |
| | 3.590 - 3.600 | Narrow-band modes - automatically controlled data stations (unattended) |
| 3.600 - 3.800 | | Phone ie SSB (and Morse) |
| | 3.600 - 3.620 | All modes - automatically controlled data stations (unattended) |
| | 3.600 - 3.650 | Preferred section for phone contest contacts |
| | 3.663 | May be used for UK emergency communications traffic |
| | 3.690 | QRP SSB centre of activity |
| | 3.700 - 3.800 | Preferred section for phone contest contacts |
| | 3.735 | Image modes centre of activity |
| | 3760 | IARU Region 1 Emergency centre of activity |
| | 3.775 - 3.800 | Priority for inter-continental contacts |

Table 6.2. 80 metres (3.5 - 3.8 MHz).

| UK Band Plan Frequencies (MHz) | | Usage |
|---|---|---|
| 10.100 - 10.140 | | Morse |
| | 10.116 | QRP centre of activity |
| 10.140 - 10.150 | | Narrow-band modes |
| NB: Automatically controlled data stations (unattended) should avoid the use of the 10MHz band. | | |

Table 6.4. 30 metres (10.100 - 10.150MHz).

including Morse and digimodes should be used. Similarly the band is not used for contests. However, 30m can be particularly interesting. Being slightly higher in frequency than 40m, longer distances are possible during the day. Often it can be a good hunting ground because it is not as heavily used as many of the other more established bands. The UK 30m band plan is shown in **Table 6.4**.

### 14.00 - 14.35MHz (20m)

This is undoubtedly the major long-haul band for radio amateurs. Although it is affected by the time of day, season and the sunspot cycle, it is possible to hear long-distance stations at most times of the day, although it may close late at night. During the day stations up to distances of around 3000km away are generally heard, although it is by no

means uncommon to hear stations much further afield at night. However, late at night few signals may be heard, especially during the winter and at the period around the sunspot minimum. Dusk and dawn also provide times when long-distance stations may be heard.

In view of its popularity, the level of interference from other stations may be high. However, this does mean that there are plenty of stations on the band and there is always the possibility of hearing distant or interesting stations. The UK 20m band plan is shown in **Table 6.5**.

### 18.068 - 18.168MHz (17m)

This is another of the bands released for amateur use after the WARC in 1979. It is only 100kHz wide but, despite its small bandwidth, many people find that it is a worthwhile band capable of producing good results. The propagation conditions are fairly similar to those on 20m although, being higher in frequency, the conditions tend to be a little better in the day and it closes earlier at night. It is also affected more by the position in the sunspot cycle. The UK 17m band plan is shown in **Table 6.6**.

### 21.00 - 21.45MHz (15m)

This is a very popular band. Being higher than 20m it is affected more by the state of the sun, and is more variable. Often it will close at night and during the periods of the sunspot minimum no amateur stations may be audible. However, the signal strengths of long-distance stations are generally a little higher than those on 20m. To gain a quick view of whether the band might be open it is possible to listen to the broadcast band that starts right at the top end of the amateur band. If signals can be heard here then there is a good possibility that amateur signals may be present.

The band is wider than any of the lower-frequency allocations. This can be a distinct advantage at times of

| UK Band Plan Frequencies (MHz) | | Usage |
|---|---|---|
| 14.000 - 14.070 | | Morse |
| | 14.000 - 14.060 | Contest preferred |
| | 14.055 | QRS (slow telegraphy) centre of activity |
| | 14.060 | QRP centre of activity |
| 14.070 - 14.099 | | Narrow band modes |
| | 14.089 - 14.099 | Narrow-band modes - automatically controlled data stations (unattended) |
| 14.099 - 14.101 | | Beacons only |
| 14.101 - 14.112 | | All modes including automatically controlled data stations (unattended) |
| 14.112 - 14.350 | | All modes |
| | 14.112 - 14.125 | All modes except digimodes |
| | 14.125 - 14.300 | Preferred section for SSB contests |
| | 14.195 ±5kHz | Priority for DXpeditions |
| | 14.230 | Image centre of activity |
| | 14.285 | QRP centre of activity |
| | 14.300 | Global emergency centre of activity |

Table 6.5. 20 metres (14.0 - 14.35MHz).

| UK Band Plan Frequencies (MHz) | | Usage |
|---|---|---|
| 18.068 - 18.095 | | Morse |
| 18.095 - 18.109 | | Narrow-band modes |
| | 18.105 - 18.109 | Narrow-band modes - automatically controlled data stations (unattended) |
| 18.109 - 18.111 | | Beacons only |
| 18.111 - 18.168 | | All modes |
| | 18.111 - 18.120 | All modes - automatically controlled data stations (unattended) |
| | 18.160 | Global emergency centre of activity |

Table 6.6. 17 metres (18.068 - 18.168MHz).

| UK Band Plan Frequencies | Usage | |
|---|---|---|
| 21.000 - 21.070 | | Morse |
| | 21.055 | QRS centre of activity |
| | 21.060 | QRP centre of activity |
| 21.070 - 21.110 | | Narrow-band modes |
| | 21.090 - 21.110 | Narrow-band modes - automatically controlled data stations (unattended) |
| 21.110 - 21.120 | | All modes (excluding SSB) |
| 21.120 - 21.149 | | Narrow-band modes |
| 21.149 - 21.151 | | Beacons only |
| 21.151 - 21.450 | | Phone (and Morse) |
| | 21.285 | QRP centre of activity |
| | 21.340 | Image centre of activity |
| | 21.360 | Global emergency centre of activity |

Table 6.7. 15 metres (21.0 - 21.45MHz).

| UK Band Plan Frequencies (MHz) | Usage | |
|---|---|---|
| 24.890 - 24.915 | | Morse |
| | 24.906 | QRP centre of activity |
| 24.915 - 24.929 | | Narrow-band modes |
| | 24.925 - 24.929 | Narrow-band modes - automatically controlled data stations (unattended) |
| 24.929 - 24.931 | | Beacons only |
| 24.931 - 24.990 | | All modes |
| | 24.931 - 24.940 | All modes - automatically controlled data stations (unattended) |

Table 6.8. 12 Metres (24.890 - 24.990 MHz)

| UK Band Plan Frequencies (MHz) | Usage | |
|---|---|---|
| 28.000 - 28.070 | | Morse |
| | 28.055 | QRS centre of activity |
| | 28.060 | QRP centre of activity |
| 28.070 - 28.190 | | Narrow band modes |
| | 28.120 - 28.150 | Narrow-band modes - automatically controlled data stations (unattended) |
| 28.190 - 28.225 | Beacons | |
| | 28.190 - 28.199 | Regional time-shared beacons |
| | 28.199 - 28.201 | World-wide time-shared beacons |
| | 28.201 - 28.225 | Continuous duty beacons |
| 28.225 - 29.300 | | All modes |
| | 28.225 - 28.300 | Beacons |
| | 28.300 - 28.320 | All modes - automatically controlled data stations (unattended) |
| | 28.360 | QRP centre of activity |
| | 28.680 | Image centre of activity |
| | 29.200 - 29.300 | All modes - automatically controlled data stations (unattended) |
| | 29.210 | UK Internet voice gateway (unattended) |
| | 29.290 | UK Internet voice gateway (unattended) |
| 29.300 - 29.510 | | Satellite downlinks |
| 29.510 - 29.520 | | Guard channel |
| 29.520 - 29.700 | | All modes |
| | 29.520 - 29.550 | FM simplex (10kHz channels) |
| | 29.530 | UK Internet voice gateway (unattended) |
| | 29.560 - 29.590 | FM repeater inputs (RH1 - RH4) |
| | 29.600 | FM calling channel |
| | 29.610 - 29.650 | FM simplex (10kHz channels) |
| | 29.630 | UK Internet voice gateway (unattended) |
| | 29.660 - 29.700 | FM repeater outputs (RH1 - RH4) |

Table 6.9. 10 metres (28.0 - 29.7MHz)

high activity, and especially during contests. The UK 15m band plan is shown in **Table 6.7**.

### 24.89 - 24.99MHz (12m)

12m is another band released after the WARC in 1979. It is relatively narrow, but nevertheless it can be a good band when the propagation conditions are favourable. However, being relatively high in frequency, the propagation conditions are very dependent upon the state of the solar cycle.

In periods of low sunspot activity the band may not open during the day and no signals may be audible. However, when conditions are good signals can be heard from far away at good strengths. It is a good hunting ground for those people with low-power stations or antennas that are not particularly high.

Being high in frequency also means that it is generally a daytime band. Signals fall away in strength after dark, and in the morning it takes a while for the level of ionisation to build up and for many long distance signals to emerge. The UK 12m band plan is shown in **Table 6.8**.

### 28.00 - 29.70MHz (10m)

This is the highest in frequency of the true short-wave or HF bands. It is situated just below the upper limit of the HF portion of the spectrum. The band is renowned for being very good when it is open, but extremely dependent upon the state of the sun. During the low part of the sunspot cycle very few signals are heard, but as the sunspot numbers start to rise, so the conditions on the band improve.

Like 12m it is essentially a daytime band, but at the peak of the sunspot cycle it may remain open after dark. When the band is open signals from all over the world can be heard at very good strengths, and those with moderate stations can easily make many good contacts. During the low part of the sunspot cycle, Sporadic E is experienced and

| UK Band Plan Frequencies (MHz) | | Usage |
|---|---|---|
| 50.000 - 50.100 | | Morse |
| | 50.000 - 50.080 | Beacons only |
| | 50.090 | Morse centre of activity |
| 50.100 - 50.500 | | All narrow-band modes (max bandwidth 2.7kHz) |
| | 50.100 - 50.130 | DX window for telegraphy and SSB (intercontinental activity only) |
| | 50.110 | Intercontinental calling frequency |
| | 50.150 | SSB centre of activity |
| | 50.185 | Cross-band centre of activity |
| | 50.250 | PSK31 centre of activity |
| 50.500 - 52.000 | | All modes |
| | 50.510 | Slow scan television |
| | 50.520 | Internet voice gateway |
| | 50.530 | Internet voice gateway |
| | 50.540 | Internet voice gateway |
| | 50.550 | Fax working frequency |
| | 50.600 | RTTY (FSK) |
| | 50.620 - 50.750 | Digital communications |
| | 50.710 - 50.910 | FM repeater outputs |
| | 51.210 | Emergency communications priority |
| | 51.210 - 51.410 | FM Repeater inputs |
| | 51.430 - 51.590 | FM telephony |
| | 51.530 | GB2RS news broadcasts and slow Morse transmissions |
| | 51.910 - 51.950 | Internet voice gateways (10 kHz channels) |
| | 51.950 - 51.990 | Emergency communications priority |

Table 6.10. 6 metres (50.0 - 52.0MHz)

| UK Band Plan Frequencies (MHz) | | Usage |
|---|---|---|
| 70.000 - 70.050 | | Beacons only |
| | 70.030 | Personal beacons |
| 70.050 - 70.250 | | Narrow-band modes |
| | 70.085 | PSK31 centre of activity |
| | 70.150 | Meteor scatter calling |
| | 70.185 | Cross-band activity centre |
| | 70.200 | SSB / Morse calling frequency |
| 70.250 - 70.294 | | All modes |
| | 70.260 | AM / FM calling |
| 70.294 - 70.500 | | All modes, channelised operation using 12.5kHz spacing |
| | 70.3000 | RTTY / fax calling frequency |
| | 70.3125 | Digital modes |
| | 70.3250 | DX Cluster |
| | 70.3375 | Digital modes |
| | 70.3500 | Internet gateway - can be used for emergency communications |
| | 70.3625 | Internet voice gateway |
| | 70.3750 | Can be used for emergency communications |
| | 70.3875 | Internet voice gateway |
| | 70.4000 | Can be used for emergency communications |
| | 70.4125 | Internet voice gateway |
| | 70.4250 | FM simplex - used by GB2RS news bulletins |
| | 70.4375 | Digital modes (special projects) |
| | 70.4500 | FM calling |
| | 70.4625 | Digital modes |
| | 70.4875 | Digital modes |

Table 6.11. 4 metres (70.0 - 70.50MHz).

gives the possibility of some long-distance contacts. Being a very wide band (1.7MHz), the levels of interference are generally lower. The bandwidth also gives the opportunity to use other types of transmission. At the high-frequency end of the band, FM operation takes place and there are even some repeaters. In addition to this a section of the band is reserved for satellite operation. All of these aspects make 10m very interesting both in terms of the propagation that can be experienced and the variety of ways in which communications can be established. The UK 10m band plan is shown in **Table 6.9**.

## 50 - 52MHz (6m)

This is the lowest of the VHF bands, being very close in frequency to the HF portion of the spectrum. At the peak of the sunspot cycle world-wide communication is possible, with long-distance stations being heard at very good strength. However, at either side of the peak when the ionosphere does not support propagation at these frequencies, distances are normally much shorter and the band takes on a feel more akin to that of the other VHF bands. Even under these conditions Sporadic E gives the possibility of long-distance contacts. The UK 6m band plan is shown in **Table 6.10**.

## 70.0 - 70.5MHz (4m)

This band of frequencies is only available for amateur operation in a very limited number of countries, of which the UK is one. (Details of the countries where it is available can be found at www.70mhz.org) However, it has been recognised that an amateur band on this frequency would be of great benefit to the amateur community and there is a possibility that in the future this allocation might be more widespread.

Since there are very few countries active on the band there is little commercial equipment available, and this

**UK Band Plan**

| Frequencies (MHz) | | Usage |
|---|---|---|
| 144.000 - 144.110 | | Telegraphy (Morse) |
| | 144.000 - 144.035 | Moonbounce (EME) exclusive |
| | 144.050 | Telegraphy calling |
| | 144.100 | Random MS telegraphy calling |
| 144.110 - 144.150 | | Narrow band modes |
| | 144.138 | PSK31 centre of activity |
| | 144.120 - 144.150 | Moonbounce (EME) machine-generated Morse |
| 144.150 - 144.180 | | Narrow-band modes |
| | 144.150 - 144.160 | FAI and Moonbounce (EME) activity SSB |
| 144.180 - 144.360 | | Telegraphy and SSB |
| | 144.175 | Microwave talk-back (for use when making Microwave contacts) |
| | 144.195 - 144.205 | Random MS SSB |
| | 144.200 | Random MS SSB calling frequency |
| | 144.250 | GB2RS news broadcast and slow Morse |
| | 144.260 | Can be used by Raynet |
| | 144.300 | SSB calling |
| 144.360 - 144.399 | | Telegraphy, MGM, SSB |
| | 144.370 | Machine-generated Morse calling frequency |
| 144.400 - 144.490 | | Propagation Beacons only |
| 144.490 - 144.500 | | (Guard band) |
| 144.500 - 144.794 | | All Modes |
| | 144.500 | SSTV calling |
| | 144.525 | ATV SSB talk-back |
| | 144.600 | RTTY calling |
| | 144.600 | RTTY working (FSK) |
| | 144.625 - 144.675 | Can be used by Raynet |
| | 144.700 | FAX calling |
| | 144.750 | Amateur television talk-back |
| | 144.775 - 144.794 | Can be used by Raynet |
| 144.794 - 144.990 | | Machine-generated Morse and Packet radio |
| | 144.800 - 144.9875 | Digital modes (including unattended) |
| | 144.8000 | Unconnected nets: APRS, *UiView* etc |
| | 144.8250 | Internet voice gateway |
| | 144.8375 | Internet voice gateway |
| | 144.8500 | AX25 BBS user access |
| | 144.8625 | Available for nodes and BBSs on application |
| | 144.8750 | TCP/IP user access |
| | 144.8875 | AX25, priority for DX Cluster access |
| | 144.9000 | AX25 DX Cluster access |
| | 144.9250 | TCP/IP user access |
| | 144.9500 | AX25 Bulletin Board System (BBS) user access |
| | 144.9750 | High speed 25kHz channel |
| 144.990 - 145.1935 | | FM RV48 - RV63 Repeater input exclusive |
| 145.200 | | FM Space communications (eg International Space Station) Earth to Space |
| 145.200 | | Can be used by Raynet |
| 145.200 - 145.5935 | | FM V16 - V48 FM simplex |
| | 145.2125 | Internet voice gateway |
| | 145.2250 | Can be used by Raynet |
| | 145.2375 | Internet voice gateway |
| | 145.2500 | Used for slow Morse transmissions |
| | 145.2875 | Internet voice gateway |
| | 145.3000 | RTTY local |
| | 145.3375 | Internet voice gateway |
| | 145.5000 | Mobile calling |
| | 145.5250 | Used for GB2RS news broadcast |
| | 145.5500 | Used for rally/exhibition talk-in |
| 145.5935 - 145.7935 | | FM RV48 - RV63 Repeater output |
| 145.800 | | FM Space communications (eg International Space Station) Space to Earth |
| 144.806 - 146.000 | | All Modes, Satellite exclusive |

**Table 6.12. 2 metres (144.0 - 146.00MHz).**

| Frequency | Channel designation | | Frequency | Channel designation | |
|---|---|---|---|---|---|
| 145.000 | RV48 (R0) | | 145.4125 | V33 | |
| 145.0125 | RV49 | | 145.425 | V34 (S17) | |
| 145.025 | RV50 (R1) | | 145.4375 | V35 | SIMPLEX |
| 145.0375 | RV51 | | 145.450 | V36 (S18) | CHANNELS |
| 145.050 | RV52 (R2) | | 145.4625 | V37 | (Cont) |
| 145.0625 | RV53 | REPEATER | 145.475 | V38 (S19) | |
| 145.075 | RV54 (R3) | INPUT | 145.4875 | V39 | |
| 145.0875 | RV55 | CHANNELS | 145.500 | V40 (S20) Calling channel | |
| 145.100 | RV56 (R4) | | 145.5125 | V41 | |
| 145.1125 | RV57 | | 145.525 | V42 (S21) | |
| 145.125 | RV58 (R5) | | 145.5375 | V43 | |
| 145.1375 | RV59 | | 145.550 | V44 (S22) | |
| 145.150 | RV60 (R6) | | 145.5625 | V45 | |
| 145.1625 | RV61 | | 145.575 | V46 (S23) | |
| 145.175 | RV62 (R7) | | 145.5875 | V47 | |
| | | | | | |
| 145.200 | V16 (S8) | | 145.600 | RV48 (R0) | |
| 145.2125 | V17 | | 145.6125 | RV49 | |
| 145.225 | V18 (S9) | | 145.625 | RV50 (R1) | |
| 145.2375 | V19 | | 145.6375 | RV51 | |
| 145.250 | V20 (S10) | | 145.650 | RV52 (R2) | |
| 145.2625 | V21 | | 145.6625 | RV53 | |
| 145.275 | V22 (S11) | | 145.675 | RV54 (R3) | REPEATER |
| 145.2875 | V23 | SIMPLEX | 145.6875 | RV55 | OUTPUT |
| 145.300 | V24 (S12) | CHANNELS | 145.700 | RV56 (R4) | CHANNELS |
| 145.3125 | V25 | | 145.7125 | RV57 | |
| 145.325 | V26 (S13) | | 145.725 | RV58 (R5) | |
| 145.3375 | V27 | | 145.7375 | RV59 | |
| 145.350 | V28 (S14) | | 145.750 | RV60 (R6) | |
| 145.3625 | V28 | | 145.7625 | RV61 | |
| 145.375 | V30 (S15) | | 145.775 | RV62 (R7) | |
| 145.3875 | V31 | | 145.7875 | RV63 | |
| 145.400 | V32 (S16) | | | | |

Table 6.13. 2 metre FM channel designations (characters in brackets refer to older 25 kHz spaced channel designations that may be heard on occasions).

results in most of the equipment being either home built or ex-mobile radio equipment (from taxis etc) that has been modified for the band. This makes 4m very interesting and appealing to many.

Propagation is very much like that found on 50MHz although normal ionospheric propagation is rarely experienced. Sporadic E does produce some excellent results when it appears, although contacts with other countries often have to be on a cross-band basis, with stations from outside the UK transmitting on either 50MHz or 28MHz. The UK 4m band plan is shown in **Table 6.11**.

### 144 - 146MHz (2m)
This is the most popular of the VHF and UHF bands, especially where FM local and mobile operation is concerned. There is a comprehensive set of 2m repeaters that together cover large parts of the UK. There is also a large level of data (packet radio) activity. For those interested in long-distance contacts there is also SSB and Morse activity which rises significantly during contests or when propagation conditions are good.

The ranges that can be achieved often depend very largely on the antenna, transmitter power and location. However, for most stations distances of at least 30 to 50km should be possible.

Those with high powers, good antennas and a good location will be able to reach much greater distances, especially when using SSB or Morse. When conditions on the band improve as a result of tropospheric propagation, distances up to 1000km can be reached on occasions, and with Sporadic E it is possible to make contacts over distances of some 2000km. However, this is the highest frequency amateur band where Sporadic E can be experienced. The UK 2m band plan is shown in **Table 6.12**.

Operation on FM is channelised. This makes it much easier to locate a particular frequency, especially when operating mobile. It also reduces the level of interference because channels are spaced such that a station on one channel does not interfere with one on the next. Channels are identified by letters and numbers as shown in **Table 6.13**. A system of channels spaced by

**UK Band Plan**

| Frequencies (MHz) | Usage | |
|---|---|---|
| 430.0000 - 431.9810 | | All modes |
| | 430.0125 - 430.0750 | Internet voice gateways (Notes 7, 8) (12.5kHz channels) |
| | 430.1625 - 430.1875 | Experimental MPT1327 Base Tx Ch 1 - 3 (12,5kHz channels) |
| | 430.4000 - 430.5750 | Digital links |
| | 430.6000 - 430.9250 | Digital repeaters |
| | 430.8000 | Raynet 7.6MHz talk-through - mobile Tx |
| | 430.8250 - 430.9750 | RU66 - RU78 7.6MHz split repeaters - outputs |

*Licence exclusion: 431 - 432MHz not available for use within a radius of 100km of Charing Cross, London*

| Frequencies (MHz) | Usage | |
|---|---|---|
| | 430.9900 - 431.9000 | Digital communications |
| | 431.0750 - 431.1750 | Internet voice gateway (6dBW max)(12.5kHz channels) |
| 432.0000 - 432.1000 | | Telegraphy (Morse) and machine-generated Morse |
| | 432.0000 - 432.0250 | Moonbounce (EME) |
| | 432.0500 | Telegraphy centre of activity |
| | 432.0880 | PSK31 centre of activity |
| 432.1000 - 432.4000 | | SSB, telegraphy and machine-generated Morse |
| | 432.2000 | SSB centre of activity |
| | 432.3500 | Microwave talk-back calling frequency (Europe) |
| | 432.3700 | FSK441 calling frequency |
| 432.4000 - 432.5000 | | Beacons exclusive |
| 432.5000 - 432.9940 | | All modes (non-channelised operation) |
| | 432.5000 | Narrow-band SSTV activity centre |
| | 432.5000 - 432.6000 | IARU Region 1 linear transponder inputs |
| | 432.6000 | RTTY (ASK/PSK) activity centre |
| | 432.6000 - 432.8000 | IARU Region 1 linear transponder outputs |
| | 432.6250 - 432.6750 | Digital communications (25 kHz channels) |
| | 432.7000 | Fax activity centre |
| | 432.7750 | Raynet 1.6MHz talk-through - base Tx |
| | 432.8000 - 432.9900 | Beacons |
| 432.9940 - 433.3810 | | FM repeater outputs (UK only) |
| | 433.0000 - 433.3750 | (RB0 - RB15) RU240 - RU270 |
| 433.3940 - 433.5810 | | FM Simplex channels |
| | 433.4250 | U274 |
| | 433.4500 | U276 |
| | 433.4750 | U278 |
| | 433.5000 | U280 (FM calling channel) |
| | 433.5250 | U282 |
| | 433.5500 | U284 (Used for rally/exhibition talk-in) |
| | 433.5750 | U286 |
| 433.6000 - 434.0000 | | All modes |
| | 433.6000 | U288 (RTTY AFSK) |
| | 433.6250 - 433.6750 | Digital communications (25kHz channels) |
| | 433.7000 | Can be used by Raynet |
| | 433.7250 - 433.7750 | Can be used by Raynet |
| | 433.8000 - 434.2500 | Digital communications |
| 433.9500 - 434.0500 | 25kHz Internet voice gateway channels | |
| | 434.0625 - 434.0875 | Experimental MPT1327 mobile Tx Ch 1 - 3 (12.5kHz channels) |
| | 434.3750 | Raynet 1.6MHz talk-through - mobile Tx |
| | 434.4750 - 434.5250 | Internet voice gateway (25kHz channels) |
| 434.5940 - 434.9810 | | FM repeater inputs (UK only) |
| 434.6000 - 434.9750 | (RB0 - RB15) RU240 - RU270 | |
| 435.0000 - 438.0000 | | Satellites and fast scan TV |
| 438.0000 - 440.0000 | | All modes |
| | 438.0250 - 438.1750 | IARU Region 1 Digital communications |
| | 438.4000 | Raynet 7.6MHz talk-through - base Tx |
| | 438.4250 - 438.5750 | RU66 - RU78 7.6 split repeaters - inputs |
| | 439.6000 - 440.0000 | Digital communications |

**Table 6.14. 70cm (430 - 440MHz).**

12.5kHz is replacing the previous one where channels were spaced by 25kHz. The designations for the old channels are shown in brackets.

## 430 - 440MHz (70cm)

Like 2m this band is very popular for local and mobile communications. There is an excellent network of repeaters in the UK and many other countries, enabling a good variety of contacts to be made even with low-power hand-held or mobile equipment.

Contacts can be made at distances of 30km and more with an average fixed station, and more if good antennas are used. For those wanting to make longer-distance contacts, SSB and Morse are better than FM. Although activity levels on these modes are often low, they increase dramatically during contests or when conditions are good.

Tropospheric propagation is the most commonly used way in which long-distance contacts are made, although other techniques including satellites and moonbounce can be tried. However, moonbounce is really a specialised technique.

The band plan for 70cm (**Table 6.14**) is somewhat more complicated than some of the lower-frequency bands, and this represents the diversity of use. There are also differences across Europe, and some of these differences need to be accommodated within the band plans.

Like 2m, 70cm has a large amount of FM operation for which channels are assigned. These have a similar method for assigning the channel designations (**Table 6.15**). Although operation is not currently migrating to a channel spacing of 12.5kHz, new designations are being introduced that can accommodate this spacing. Again, the old channel designations are shown in brackets. Most repeater operation uses a 1.6MHz spacing between input and output channels, although some are expected to use the 7.6MHz split more commonly used on mainland Europe.

| Frequency | Channel designation | | |
|---|---|---|---|
| 433.000 | RU240 (RB0) | | |
| 433.025 | RU242 (RB1) | | |
| 433.050 | RU244 (RB2) | | |
| 433.075 | RU246 (RB3) | | |
| 433.100 | RU248 (RB4) | | |
| 433.125 | RU250 (RB5) | | |
| 433.150 | RU252 (RB6) | | |
| 433.175 | RU254 (RB7) | | REPEATER |
| 433.200 | RU256 (RB8) | | OUTPUT |
| 433.225 | RU258 (RB9) | | CHANNELS |
| 433.250 | RU260 (RB10) | | |
| 433.275 | RU262 (RB11) | | |
| 433.300 | RU264 (RB12) | | |
| 433.325 | RU266 (RB13) | | |
| 433.350 | RU268 (RB14) | | |
| 433.375 | RU270 (RB15) | | |
| | | | |
| 433.400 | U272 (SU16) | | |
| 433.425 | U274 (SU17) | | |
| 433.450 | U276 (SU18) | | |
| 433.475 | U278 (SU19) | | |
| 433.500 | U280 (SU20) | (Calling channel) | SIMPLEX |
| 433.525 | U282 (SU21) | | CHANNELS |
| 433.550 | U284 (SU22) | | |
| 433.575 | U286 (SU23) | | |
| 433.600 | U288 (SU24) | | |
| | | | |
| 434.600 | RU240 (RB0) | | |
| 434.625 | RU242 (RB1) | | |
| 434.650 | RU244 (RB2) | | |
| 434.675 | RU246 (RB3) | | |
| 434.700 | RU248 (RB4) | | |
| 434.725 | RU250 (RB5) | | |
| 434.750 | RU252 (RB6) | | |
| 434.775 | RU254 (RB7) | | REPEATER |
| 434.800 | RU256 (RB8) | | INPUT |
| 434.825 | RU258 (RB9) | | CHANNELS |
| 434.850 | RU260 (RB10) | | |
| 434.875 | RU262 (RB11) | | |
| 434.900 | RU264 (RB12) | | |
| 434.925 | RU266 (RB13) | | |
| 434.950 | RU268 (RB14) | | |
| 434.975 | RU270 (RB15) | | |

Table 6.15. 70 cm FM channel designations.

## MICROWAVES

Above 432MHz there are many other bands that provide further areas for experimentation and interest. Often activity on these bands is somewhat less, and the technical challenges are a little greater. Nevertheless these bands should not be forgotten, and it is well worth taking a look on them to see if operation on these frequencies appeals. Unfortunately space in this book limits a complete description of every band. More details of microwave band plans etc can be found on the RSGB website and in other RSGB publications.

## BEACONS

Propagation conditions can change significantly over a short period of time. Whilst there are many computer programs that are able to predict what conditions may be like there is no substitute for actually listening to see which paths are open. One of the most reliable methods of achieving this is to have a beacon station transmitting all the time. On 10m and the VHF and UHF bands there are several stations that do just this. However, another international system has been set up and is active on a number of the HF bands including 10, 15 and 20m, and it is being extended to other bands. Here stations all around the world are co-ordinated and transmit one after the other. They identify themselves and then transmit on three decreasing power levels before passing on to the next station. This means that only one frequency has to be monitored to gain a very good appreciation of band conditions. These beacons can be found at the centre of the 2kHz wide beacon allocations on the HF bands.

## NOTE ON USE OF BAND PLANS

It is emphasised that the band plans presented here are examples of the UK band plans that were current in 2006, and that it is important always to use the most recent band plan issued for your country. The current UK band plans are available on the RSGB Spectrum Forum website, and there is a link from the main RSGB site. Both website addresses are given in 'Further Information' below.

---

### FURTHER INFORMATION

*Radio Propagation – Principles and Practice*, Ian Poole, G3YWX, RSGB, 2004.
*Guide to VHF/UHF Amateur Radio*, Ian Poole, G3YWX, RSGB, 2000.
*Amateur Radio Operating Manual*, 6th edn, Don Field, G3XTT (ed), RSGB, 2004.
*RSGB Yearbook*, Steve White, G3ZVW (ed) published annually by the RSGB.
RSGB website (home page): www.rsgb.org
RSGB Spectrum Forum website (current UK band plans): www.rsgb-spectrumforum.org.uk/rsgb_bandplan.htm

---

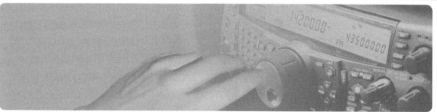

# 7. On the Bands

Photo: 9M6DXX

**A modern transceiver covering all amateur radio bands from 1.8 to 50MHz.**

**W**HEN LISTENING ON the bands it can take a short time to 'learn the ropes' of what goes on. Topics like finding out how contacts are made, how to make the best use of the time spent, knowing how to search out the more interesting stations, what contests are and how to participate in them, how to operate through repeaters and the like are all important and they form the basic operating skills any listener or transmitting amateur should know. They enable people to gain the most enjoyment out of the hobby and to use their equipment to the best, whether chasing stations at the other side of the world or having local chats across town.

## LISTEN, LISTEN, LISTEN

One of the most useful pieces of advice ever given to someone who had recently gained his licence was to "listen, listen and then listen some more" before transmitting. Even prior to gaining a transmitting licence, listening is very useful because it enables you to find out at first hand how to conduct a contact, use technology like repeaters and so forth. It helps refine and develop the skills that will be so useful when transmitting, and above all it can be fascinating to listen on the bands to find out what is going on.

There is a great temptation when you are able to transmit just to put out CQ calls and expect interesting stations to reply. But by far the best way is to seek out those stations you want to contact by listening on the bands and then calling *them*. It requires a little more restraint but it is far more successful.

## BASIC CONTACTS

Many of the contacts that take place on the short-wave bands are what are termed 'rubber stamp' contacts, consisting of the minimum amount of information. These are a good starting place for many people. Especially when starting out on the air it is useful to know what to say. Also for those people who do not speak English as their first language it is relatively easy to have a contact using a minimum vocabulary. However, many people like to talk about far more than is contained within the basic contact. Often technical discussions may be heard, or stations may be describing the part of the world where they live. Whilst some will want to have long contacts and discussions, it is important to know the basic elements of a contact first.

On the HF bands a contact will often start off with a 'CQ' or general call. A formula known as 'three times three' is a good starting point. The letters "CQ", meaning that you want to have a contact ("seek you"), are repeated three times, and then the callsign (usually in phonetics) is repeated three times. This whole procedure is repeated three times. In this way the call is kept to a reasonable length and anyone listening is able to gain the callsign and the fact that a contact is wanted. See **Table 7.1** for an example of a typical phone contact.

Any station listening who wants a contact can then respond when invited to do so. He will normally give his callsign a couple of times using phonetics and then invite the other station to transmit.

If the first station hears the caller and responds, he will announce the callsigns and then normally wish him good day and then give a signal report. This is very useful. Not only does it tell the other station how he is being received and can give information about his station's

Hello CQ CQ CQ, this is G3YWX, Golf three Yankee Whisky Xray, Golf three Yankee Whisky Xray, CQ CQ CQ, this is G3YWX, Golf three Yankee Whisky Xray, Golf three Yankee Whisky Xray, CQ CQ CQ, this is G3YWX, Golf three Yankee Whisky Xray, Golf three Yankee Whisky Xray, and G3YWX, Golf three Yankee Whisky Xray is standing by for a call.

G3YWX, Golf three Yankee Whisky Xray, this is GW8FEO, Golf Whisky eight Foxtrot Echo Oscar, Golf Whisky eight Foxtrot Echo Oscar.

GW8FEO, this is G3YWX. Good morning old man and thank you for the call. Your report is 5 and 9, 5 and 9. My name is Ian, India Alpha November, Ian, and the location is Staines, Sierra Tango Alpha India November Echo Sierra. So how do you copy? G3XDV this is G3YWX listening.

G3YWX here is GW8FEO. Good morning Ian and thank you for the report. Your report is 5 and 9 as well. My name is Steve, Sierra Tango Echo Victor Echo, and I am located at Rhyl, Romeo Hotel Yankee Lima, on the north coast of Wales. So I'll pass it back to you and see how you copy. G3YWX this is GW8FEO passing transmission back to you

GW8FEO this is G3YWX. Thank you very much for the report Steve, and it is good to talk to you for the first time. The equipment here is a small transceiver running about 50 watts and the antenna is a vertical. The weather here today is hot and sunny, about 23 degrees, although we did have a little rain earlier. So I wonder how you are copying? GW8FEO here is G3YWX.

G3YWX this is GW8FEO. Fine business Ian and your transmitter is doing a good job for you. I am running about 100 watts to a dipole at about 10 metres. The weather here is cold and wet, about 15 degrees, but it should improve. So back to you, G3YWX here is GW8FEO.

GW8FEO here is G3YWX. Fine there Steve, and your equipment is also doing a good job for you. I would like to exchange QSL cards. I will send mine via the bureau and I look forward to receiving yours. I don't have a lot more to say so I will wish 73 to you and yours, and look forward to the next QSO. GW8FEO here is G3YWX listening for your final.

G3YWX this is GW8FEO. Yes OK there Ian. Thank you for the QSO. I'll certainly send a card via the bureau and look forward to receiving yours. 73 and I hope to have another contact with you further down the log. All the best. G3YWX this is GW8FEO signing.

73 Steve, G3YWX clear.

**Table 7.1. A typical contact that might be made on the short-wave bands.**

performance but, if conditions are difficult, the contact can be tailored to meet the conditions. Once the report is given it is normal to give one's name and location. Then the callsigns will be given and transmission handed over.

The second station will follow a similar format, giving a report, his name and location. On the next transmission information about equipment in the station - the transmitter and receiver or transceiver and the antenna - are often given. Details of the weather are also often mentioned. Again callsigns are given at the beginning and end of each transmission.

On the third transmission details about exchanging QSL cards may be given and then they may sign off.

Once a contact has finished it is perfectly permissible to call one of the stations. Normally the frequency 'belongs' to the person who called CQ on the frequency but, if the other station is called, he may ask to keep the frequency or move off to another one.

Giving callsigns at the beginning and end of each transmission may seem somewhat formal. It fulfils legal requirements to identify the station (exact requirements are in the licence), but it also serves to let the other station know exactly what is happening and when he is expected to transmit. Using good operating technique is very important and helps contact to be maintained with the minimum possibility of confusion, especially when conditions are poor or interference levels are high. In essence one of the keys to becoming a good operator is to let the other station know exactly what you are doing and not leave him guessing.

When a station in a very rare location is on the band, or during contests, contacts are usually kept much shorter to enable as many contacts as possible to be made. Usually the contact will consist of just the callsigns of the stations and then a report. Speedy operating is of the essence under these conditions to ensure that others are not kept waiting and as many contacts as possible are made.

When using Morse, similar contacts can be made. The main difference is that far more abbreviations are used to ensure that the speed at which information can be passed is as quick as possible. See **Table 7.2** for an example of a typical Morse contact.

Although Morse may appear to be difficult to learn, it can bring many rewards. It is often found that it is much easier for a low powered station to make good contacts using Morse. For someone owning a more average station, not using huge antennas and high powers, Morse gives the opportunity of making contacts with distant stations, or getting through pile-ups that may not be pos-

CQ CQ CQ DE G3YWX G3YWX G3YWX CQ CQ CQ DE G3YWX G3YWX G3YWX CQ CQ CQ DE G3YWX G3YWX G3YWX AR K

G3YWX DE GW8FEO GW8FEO AR KN

GW8FEO DE G3YWX GM OM ES TNX FER CALL UR RST 599 599 = NAME IS IAN IAN ES QTH STAINES STAINES = SO HW CPI? AR GW8FEO DE G3YWX KN

G3YWX DE GW8FEO FB OM ES TNX FER RPRT UR RST 599 599 = NAME IS STEVE STEVE ES QTH RHYL RHYL = SO HW? AR G3YWX DE GW8FEO KN

GW8FEO DE G3YWX FB STEVE ES TNX FER RPRT = TX RNG 30 WATTS ES ANT VERT = WX FB SUNNY ES ABT 23 C = SO HW CPI? AR GW8FEO DE G3YWX

G3YWX DE GW8FEO R R AGN IAN = RIG ERE RNG 100 WATTS ES ANT DI-POLE UP 10 METRES = WX WET ES COLD ABT 15 C = G3YWX DE GW8FEO KN

GW8FEO DE G3YWX FB STEVE ES UR RIG DOING FB. QRU = QSL VIA BURO = 73 ES HPE CUAGN SN AR GW8FEO DE G3YWX KN

G3YWX DE GW8FEO R R QRU ALSO = QSL FB VIA BURO = SO TNX FER QSO 73 ES BCNU AR G3YWX DE GW8FEO VA

GW8FEO DE G3YWX FM 73 ES BCNU AR GW8FEO DE G3YWX VA

**Table 7.2. A typical Morse contact. Note: the = sign is used as a full stop or 'break'.**

sible if SSB were used. Even though there is now no requirement to learn Morse to gain access to the HF bands in the UK, it can bring many benefits in terms of the capability of the stations.

Operation on the VHF and UHF bands using FM tends to be rather different. People are interested in longer contacts where they might talk about a wide variety of topics, technical or otherwise. A short call may be made on the calling channel to check if anyone is available for a contact. A full CQ call is rarely made, but instead a call of the form "G3YWX is listening on this channel for a contact", or possibly for a particular station. The channel is not occupied for any length of time in case others want to use the channel. Once a contact is made stations move off to another clear channel. Accordingly it is wise to check which channels might be free before making a call.

Again, callsigns should be used at the beginning an end of each trans-mission, although generally there is less emphasis on the use of the phonetic alphabet. Reports are exchanged and, if the stations have not made contact before, names and lo-cations are given. The contacts are generally less formalised than they are on the HF bands because of the prevailing conditions and the fact that people generally want to talk for longer, and often know one another better.

## REPEATERS

Repeaters are widely used on the VHF and UHF bands, where they enable stations with poor antennas and locations (eg mobile or portable stations) to make contacts over much greater distances. The repeater itself generally has a very good location, giving it a wide coverage area. Stations are able to transmit into it and their transmissions are relayed on another frequency.

According to the band in use there is a set separation between the transmit and receive frequencies. This is 500kHz on the 50MHz band, 600kHz on 145MHz, 1.6 or 7.6MHz on 433MHz, and 6MHz on 1.3GHz.

The spacing between the channels also varies according to the band in use. It is 10kHz on 50MHz, 12.5kHz on 144MHz, and on 433MHz and 1.2GHz it is 25 kHz.

Repeaters have a number of

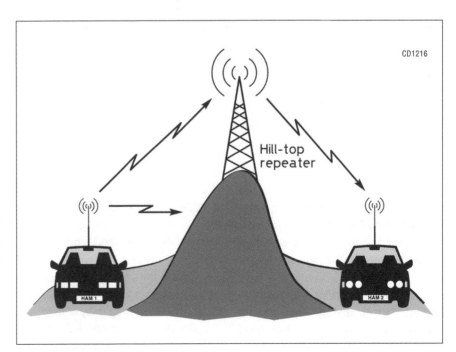

CD1216

Hill-top repeater

HAM 1     HAM 2

**Fig 7.1. Operation through a repeater.**

automatically controlled functions. These enable them to operate in a more efficient manner. This means that when operating through a repeater it is essential to have a basic knowledge of its operation so that it can be used satisfactorily.

Initially when a repeater is not in use it will not radiate a signal. To 'open' the repeater there must be a signal on its receive or 'input' frequency. This signal must be sufficiently strong for re-transmission and it must also have a tone to signify to the repeater that its transmission is to be re-radiated.

There are two methods of achieving this. The first is to use a 'tone burst' at the beginning of the transmission. An alternative to this is a system known as CTCSS (Continuous Tone Coded Squelch System), where a sub-audible tone is transmitted (this system is described later). The use of a tone burst at the beginning of a transmission is the simplest way to access a repeater. It consists of a short tone (less than a second) at the beginning of the first transmission to open the repeater. The standard frequency adopted in Europe for the tone is 1750Hz. A margin of 25Hz either way will normally access a repeater although it is wise to maintain the tone burst frequency more accurately than this.

Once the repeater has been accessed, the incoming signal will be transmitted on the output frequency. Some repeaters have a time-out facility. This monitors the time a signal has been relayed and if a certain time has been exceeded the repeater will go into a busy or time-out mode and stop retransmitting the signal. This generally occurs after about two minutes on 2m repeaters or five minutes on 70cm ones. This facility is included to discourage people from talking too long on the repeater.

When a transmission is complete the repeater will detect that the signal

has disappeared from its input. After a short delay it will transmit an audio Morse character as an invitation for the next station to transmit. This character is often a 'K'. At this point the timers are reset and a new transmission can start. However, this time no tone burst is required.

Once a contact has been completed and there are no further transmissions appearing on its input the repeater will close down. Before any further transmission can be made it will have to be re-opened.

With the rise in the number of repeaters, channels have to be re-used relatively frequently. As a result

it is sometimes possible for a station to access more than one repeater at any given time with the tone burst system described earlier. This is obviously not desirable and so the CTCSS system has been devised to overcome it. CTCSS is being increasingly used, and today most 2m and 70cm repeaters use it.

The advantage of using CTCSS tones is that by careful planning of the network, it is not possible to access two repeaters with the same CTCSS tone on the same channel. Repeaters that use CTCSS tones transmit the letter corresponding to the tone when it transmits its callsign.

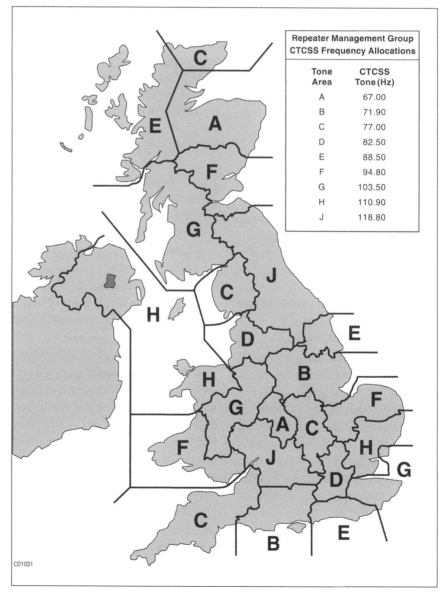

| Repeater Management Group CTCSS Frequency Allocations | |
| --- | --- |
| Tone Area | CTCSS Tone (Hz) |
| A | 67.00 |
| B | 71.90 |
| C | 77.00 |
| D | 82.50 |
| E | 88.50 |
| F | 94.80 |
| G | 103.50 |
| H | 110.90 |
| J | 118.80 |

Fig 7.2. CTCSS tones in the UK were originally planned according to this map. Most stations hold to this but there are a few exceptions.

This tone can then be programmed in to transceivers that have the CTCSS facility. It should also be noted that repeaters using CTCSS can normally still be activated using a tone burst.

Activity on repeaters is often very high. This means that it is necessary to maintain high standards of operating and, in particular, not use the repeater for too long.

There are also several procedures that are special to repeater use. The first is to note that CQ calls are not made. Instead stations announce that they are "listening through" the repeater. This can be done quickly and it is quite sufficient to enable other stations to hear anyone who is calling and then to reply. When a contact has been set up it will follow very much the same format as any other contact at VHF or UHF. Reports of how the signal is being received into the repeater as well as names and locations will be exchanged.

Once a contact has been set up it is quite possible that both stations find they can complete their contact without the use of the repeater. This is particularly true, for example, when two mobile stations are moving towards one another. If this is so, the repeater should be vacated to allow others to use it.

In addition to this, as repeaters are intended mainly for mobile stations, fixed stations should only use them when absolutely necessary and priority should be given to mobile stations.

Finally, even though all repeaters follow the same basic rules, they will vary slightly. Therefore it is always wise to listen to the repeater for a while before actually using it. If this is done few problems should be encountered.

## DXING TECHNIQUES

Many people like chasing after far-off stations or those in rare locations. It can be a real challenge to make contact with a new country when many

Photo: 9M6DXX

A scene from a DXpedition. Putting up a Yagi beam antenna at the perfect location: right on the water's edge.

other people are calling at the same time. It requires operating skill to be able to find these stations in the first place, and then to make contact against the competition.

The first stage in the process is to find the stations. There are plenty of aspects to this. The propagation conditions are obviously an important start. It is necessary to know what the conditions are like on any given band. This can be ascertained in a number of ways as discussed in the chapter on Propagation. In addition to this it is well worth listening on the bands to get a feel for what the conditions are like.

Information about special stations also appears in radio magazines and on the Internet. This will give a good idea of what to look out for. Often times and frequencies where they have been heard before are given and these offer a guide to any favoured frequencies, times and where and when they may appear in the future.

There is also a lot of skill that can be gained to help home in quickly on any interesting stations on the band. Aspects such as the operator speaking with a different accent to the rest of the stations on the band, or sounding different in some way. Also

when tuning up and down the band it is worth listening out for a 'pile-up', where many people are trying to call a particular station.

When calling someone in a pile-up it is necessary to get your call in at exactly the right time after the previous contact has finished. Rapid and exact operating is the name of the game, giving your callsign quickly and accurately. However, in the excitement it is necessary to be careful not to call too soon or out of place, thereby causing interference. Much can be learned by listening carefully before making a call.

One particular point to note is that many DX stations, especially DXpedition stations, use *split frequency* operation. They transmit on one frequency and listen on another, keeping their transmit frequency clear so that all can hear them easily. When stations operate in this manner, they announce where they are listening, so it can be particularly annoying for all trying to contact them if someone transmits without listening on the frequency of the DX station! Needless to say this does happen quite often. Obviously the DX station will not hear them as they will be listening elsewhere. Typically the split between transmit and receive may be between 2 and 5kHz for Morse operation and possibly 5 to 20kHz for SSB. Therefore it is always wise to take a little time to listen before putting in a call.

Also listen out for signals that sound 'different'. Those that come across the earth's north or south pole often have a 'watery' or 'fluttery' sound to them. It is also possible to pick up some interesting stations as the band is closing at night. At this time interference levels may be less from short-skip stations and competition from stations to the east will also be less. Also, under these conditions long-distance stations are often heard.

These and many other techniques will be learned quickly and all help the DXer to be able to make more successful contacts with rare and interesting stations.

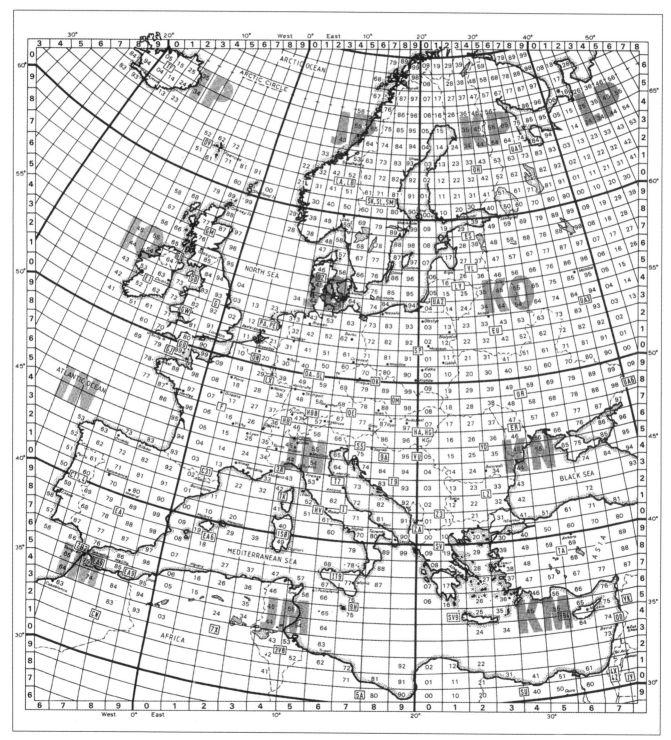

Fig 7.3. The IARU locator map for Europe showing the large and medium sized squares corresponding to the first four characters of the locator.

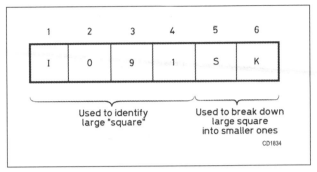

**Fig 7.4. The locator system.**

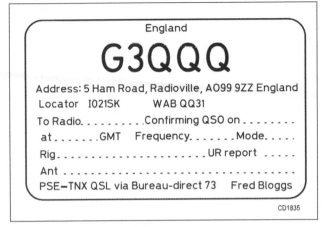

England

# G3QQQ

Address: 5 Ham Road, Radioville, AO99 9ZZ England
Locator   IO21SK       WAB QQ31
To Radio. . . . . . . . .Confirming QSO on . . . . . . . .
at . . . . . . .GMT   Frequency. . . . . . .Mode. . . . .
Rig. . . . . . . . . . . . . . . . . . . . .UR report  . . . . .
Ant . . . . . . . . . . . . . . . . . . . . . . . . . . . . . . . . .
PSE–TNX QSL via Bureau-direct 73    Fred Bloggs

CD1835

**Fig 7.5. A typical QSL card.**

## LOCATORS

One feature of VHF and UHF operation is the practice of using a 'locator' system. Essentially this enables stations to give their locations fairly accurately without having to resort to latitude and longitude. A locator map of Europe is shown in **Fig 7.3**.

The locator system approved by the International Amateur Radio Union (IARU) was developed by GM4ANB and it is called the IARU Locator or Maidenhead Locator system. It splits the world up into a matrix of main squares which occupy 20° latitude by 10° longitude. These squares are designated by two letters. The first refers to the longitude and the second the latitude, starting at 180° west and 90° south with the square 'AA' and finishing at 180° east and 90° north with 'RR'. They are the first two characters, ('IO'), in **Fig 7.4**.

These squares are each subdivided into a hundred smaller squares occupying 2° of longitude and 1° of latitude. These squares are given numeric designations starting with '00' in the south west and '99' in the north east. These two numbers occupy positions 3 and 4 in the locator ('91' in our example).

A final subdivision is made to enable the location to be fixed even more precisely. These areas are designated by letters starting with 'AA' and finishing with 'XX', and they occupy the last two positions in the locator. The size of these last areas is 5' longitude by 2.5' latitude. These are the letters 'SK' in the example shown in Fig 7.4.

## QSL CARD COLLECTING

When a contact has been made it is often nice to have it confirmed with a QSL card. These cards, deriving their name from the Q-code meaning "I confirm reception", are usually postcard sized. They contain the essential details of the contact and are often very colourful, sometimes with photographs on the front. Although there is no hard and fast rule about how a card should look or exactly how the information should be presented,

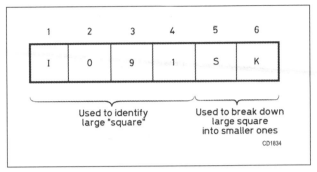

A selection of QSL cards from around the world.

it should contain certain details about the contact.

Firstly the card has the callsign of the station printed prominently on it, together with its address or location and the name of its owner. Obviously the callsign of the station with whom the contact was made is needed, along with the date and time (in GMT), the band or frequency and the mode in use. The report that was given in the contact should be included and details of the equipment are also useful. There is normally space to say whether a return QSL card is wanted and the route that can be used; typically the wording is "PSE / TNX QSL DIRECT / VIA BURO". Finally there is a space for the operator's signature.

Many people enjoy sending and receiving QSL cards and millions are sent each year. As most of them cross country borders and many are sent from one continent to another, the cost of sending them by post can be high. To help reduce costs a 'QSL bureau' system has been set up. National

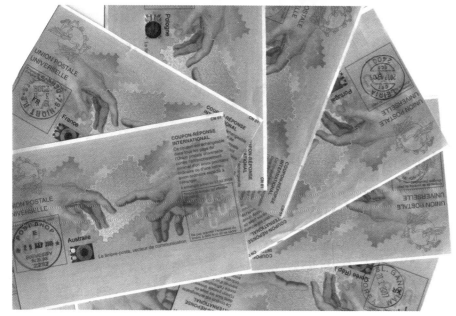

New-type (2007 issue) International Reply Coupons (IRC).

radio societies act as a collecting point and stations are able to send their cards there in bulk. The cards are sorted into countries along with those from other members, and then can be sent abroad in bulk. They are again sorted and sent to the destination station, again several at a time. Although the system does take much longer than sending them direct, ie via the post, it is very much cheaper and it is often worth the additional wait.

As some stations in remote areas of the globe may receive many thousands of cards it may not be convenient or practical for them to handle all the cards themselves. Accordingly some stations have people who act as 'QSL managers'. Normally the manager will be announced over the air and stations sending cards should direct them to the manager and not to the station directly.

As many DX stations receive many thousands of cards, those wanting a direct response should include return postage. For stations abroad this can be done using international reply coupons (IRCs). They are quite expensive but it can be worth it to get the card of a particularly rare station.

Nowadays with the increased use of the Internet, many stations are starting to use electronic QSL cards.

These save on the cost of printing and sending cards, although paper cards are still as popular as ever. Two main systems are now used: one is named Logbook of The World (LoTW), which is run by the American Radio Relay League (ARRL) and this can be located on the web at www.arrl.org/lotw The other is the Electronic QSL Card Centre, which can be located at www.eQSL.cc

## AWARDS

Another interest that many people have is to work towards gaining some of the many operating awards that are available. These present an interesting challenge in obtaining them and then they can be displayed in the radio shack. There are awards for the HF bands and for bands at VHF and above, so whatever your field of interest and class of licence there are awards available.

One of the most famous is the DX Century Club (DXCC) award (see page 3). This is awarded by the ARRL (the national amateur radio society in the USA) to people who can supply proof (QSL cards) that they have made contact with stations in at least one hundred countries. For people who have contacted more, there are endorsements that can be added. In fact some people have made contact with over 300 countries, and this represents a considerable achievement.

Another popular award that can be used to start a collection is the Worked All Continents. This is issued by the International Amateur Radio Union (IARU) and can be obtained through the RSGB. It can be gained by submitting proof of making contact with stations in six continents, namely Europe, Africa, North America, South America, Asia and Oceania.

A typical operating award.

For the VHF and UHF operator there are also many awards. As the distances that can be achieved are generally not so great there is less emphasis on making contact with different countries. For example, for the VHF Countries and Postal Districts award the number of countries and postal districts needed depends upon the band used, and on 144MHz nine countries and 65 postal districts are required for the standard award. It is also available to listeners on a 'heard' basis.

Further details of these awards are available in the *RSGB Yearbook*.

## CONTESTS

At certain times of the year the bands erupt with activity when a contest is on. Contests can be very exciting, and it is possible to contact a large number of stations from many new and interesting areas. For those on the HF bands it can be a time when a large number of new countries may be contacted, and for those on VHF and UHF new locator squares, counties and postal districts.

In most contests the idea is to contact as many other stations as possible during the time of the event. Points may be gained in a number of

A contest trophy plaque.

| Contest (and modes) | | Date | Comments |
|---|---|---|---|
| *CQ* Worked Prefixes (WPX) (RTTY) | HF | Second full W/E February | Stations contact as many stations as possible. Extra points given for new prefixes contacted. |
| ARRL DX Contest (CW) | HF | Third Full W/E February | Stations contact USA/Canada |
| ARRL DX Contest (SSB) | HF | First full W/E March | Stations contact USA/Canada |
| *CQ* Worked Prefixes (WPX) (SSB) | HF | Last full W/E March | Stations contact as many stations as possible. Extra points given for new prefixes contacted. |
| *CQ* Worked Prefixes (WPX) (CW) | HF | Last Full W/E May | Stations contact as many stations as possible. Extra points are given for new prefixes contacted. |
| CW Field Day (UK) (CW) | HF | Usually First W/E June | British portable stations make as many contacts as possible. |
| All Asia (CW) | HF | Third full W/E June | Contact stations in Asia. |
| VHF Field Day (SSB / CW) | VHF | First full W/E July | British portable stations make as many contacts as possible. Operation is mainly SSB. |
| IARU HF Championship (SSB / CW) | HF | Second full W/E July | Contact as many stations as possible. Extra points given for new countries contacted. |
| RSGB Islands On The Air (SSB/CW) | HF | Last full W/E July | Contact as many stations as possible. Extra points given for working island stations. |
| Worked All Europe DX (CW) | HF | Second full W/E August | Stations outside Europe contact as many European stations as possible. |
| All Asia (SSB) | HF | First full W/E September | Contact stations in Asia. |
| SSB Field Day (SSB) | HF | First full W/E September | Portable stations make as many contacts as possible. |
| RSGB 144MHz Trophy | VHF | First full W/E September | Many portable stations set up. Aim of contest is to make as many contacts as possible. |
| Worked All Europe DX (SSB) | HF | 2nd full W/E September | Stations outside Europe to contact as many European stations as possible. |
| *CQ* World Wide (RTTY) | HF | Fourth full W/E September | Contact as many stations in as many countries as possible. |
| IARU 432MHz - 248GHz (SSB / CW) | UHF | First W/E October | Many portable stations set up. Aim of contest is to make as many contacts as possible. |
| *CQ* World Wide (SSB) | HF | Last full W/E October | Contact as many stations in as many countries as possible. |
| Worked All Europe DX (RTTY) | HF | Second full W/E November | Stations outside Europe to contact as many European stations as possible. |
| *CQ* World Wide (CW) | HF | Last full W/E November | Contact as many stations in as many countries as possible. |

Table 7.2. Major amateur radio HF / VHF / UHF contests

ways. They may be given for each station contacted (there may be more if they are in another country or continent), and then multipliers may be given for the number of different countries or zones etc contacted. Each contest has its own rules and they differ from one to the next. A summary of the major contests is given in **Table 7.2**.

## SUMMARY

Whilst there are many types of contact there are a few guidelines that should be followed whatever the frequency band or type of contact. A radio amateur should always be polite and courteous. He / she should be helpful, and be aware of others on the air, remembering not to cause interference or use frequencies others have used first. His / her language should be clean, and subjects like

politics and religion should be avoided.

It is well worth remembering to spend plenty of time listening to find out about operating standards first. Also, listen before transmitting and find out If the frequency is in use. Whilst there is always the temptation to press the transmit button, all the best operators agree that time spent listening is very well spent.

Also remember that there are

plenty of different types of operating. Some people like DXing, others like chatting to local friends. Other people enjoy using data modes. But whatever your own brand of operating, try to explore new avenues of the hobby because there is always something new to do that can be very interesting.

Finally, operating your station is meant to be enjoyable, so do enjoy your time on the bands.

---

### FURTHER INFORMATION

Up-to-the-minute information about operating can be found each month in *RadCom*, the magazine of the Radio Society of Great Britain.
*RSGB Yearbook*, Steve White, G3ZVW (ed), RSGB (published annually).
*Amateur Radio Operating Manual*, 6th edn, Don Field, G3XTT, RSGB, 2005.
*Guide to VHF / UHF Amateur Radio*, Ian Poole, G3YWX, RSGB, 2000.
*HF Amateur Radio*, 2nd Edition, Ian Poole, G3YWX, RSGB 2007.

---

---

# 8. Receivers

An example of a 'world band' receiver.

**A** RADIO RECEIVER is the most important element in any radio station. Today there is a large variety of radios, from small transistor portable receivers, through scanners and 'world band' radios to professional communications receivers. The cost of these sets varies considerably. A high end communications receiver will cost many times that of an ordinary broadcast portable set. Its performance is also far better, being designed to meet the exacting requirements needed by the discerning user.

## CONTROLS

Each type of receiver is designed for different types of use but whatever set is available there is plenty on the bands that can be heard. However, to make the best use of the set it is necessary to know how to use it properly. Fortunately, many of the controls are similar and, once the concept behind each one is grasped, it makes operating almost any receiver very much easier.

## TUNING

Obviously the most important control on any set is the tuning control. Whilst on some sets it may be located almost anywhere on the receiver, on communications receivers it tends to be located near the centre of the front panel. This position is chosen because the receiver is generally situated on a table, and it makes for much easier use over long periods of time. The tuning knob should be able to give sufficient control to tune in the wide variety of signals that may be received. Signals such as single sideband or Morse require fine adjustments to the receiver frequency to be made because small frequency changes can make a significant difference to the signal. Modes such as FM and AM can accommodate much coarser levels of control. Some sets even have variable tune rates that can be programmed in, allowing for a fine tuning resolution where very narrow bandwidths are used and coarser tuning for wide-band modes. This makes tuning over large sections of the spectrum much easier.

The control should be smooth and not have any 'backlash'. Unfortunately it is the case that many mechanical tuning arrangements do have backlash. When the direction of tuning is reversed the 'slack' in the tuning has to be taken up before the frequency of the set itself is changed. This can be quite annoying if it is present to any degree.

## BANDSWITCH

Some receivers today do not have a bandswitch as they are able to tune continuously from one end of their frequency spectrum to the other. However, other receivers, especially older ones, have a switch for the different bands they cover. The switch is required to change the tuning ranges of the circuits being used for the particular band. A number of older receivers were 'amateur bands only' and the switch would be operated to change from one band to the next. This had the advantage that it was very easy to change bands as one operation only was required.

## KEYPAD

Today many receivers are controlled by a microprocessor and this gives a considerable amount of

Keypad on a communications receiver.

additional flexibility to these sets. To communicate with the processor and take advantage of many of these facilities a small keypad is often included as part of the front panel. Not only does this include keys for entry of numerals, but there are also special keys for controlling a number of the functions of the set.

## MEMORIES

One of the functions present on many receivers is a memory. Using this it is possible to store the frequency of a particular station. As most sets with a memory facility have a hundred or more frequencies that can be stored this means that it is possible to store a great variety of stations. For example it would be possible to store the frequencies of a group of broadcast stations that are being monitored. Often the same station broadcasts on several frequencies and, using the memory facility, it is possible to monitor each one quickly to check for the best reception.

The memory and scanning controls on a communications receiver.

## SCAN

Another facility that is present on many modern-day receivers is the ability to scan a band of frequencies. Either the set can be programmed to scan between one frequency and another, or it can be made to scan through the memory

A typical scanner.

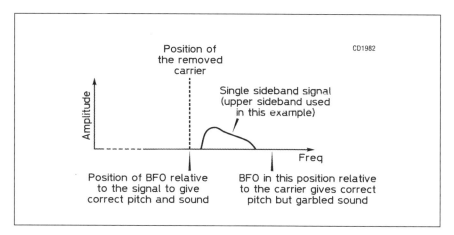

Fig 8.1. Resolving SSB.

channels, automatically stopping when a signal is found. This facility is found in all scanners and it is particularly useful when monitoring a variety of channels. Once a signal is found the set will stop whilst the transmission is present, and then continue to scan the remaining channels once the signal disappears. In this way a number of channels can be monitored very easily and the chance of missing a vital transmission is reduced.

## AF / RF GAINS

An AF gain or volume control is present on virtually every radio, and its operation is very straightforward. It is simply used to set the level of volume required to listen to the set.

Concentric AF and RF gain controls on a communications receiver.

Many sets also have an RF gain control. This is used to adjust the gain of early stages of the set. If very strong signals are present, some stages in the receiver may become overloaded. By reducing the level of gain, this can be prevented. Under normal operation most people leave the RF gain set to maximum because the best signal-to-noise ratio is ob-

tained if the gain of the first stages is maximised.

Although not common practice these days, some sets also have an IF gain control. This should be used in the same way as the RF gain control, reducing the gain of the RF stages first, then the IF stages.

## MODE SWITCH

There is a variety of modes that can be received: AM, FM, SSB and Morse are the most common. In order to be able to demodulate these different types of modulation, different circuits are required within the receiver. Some receivers, and in particular scanners, may default to a particular type of modulation for a given band, but most sets that are intended for use apart from just broadcast listening have a switch so that the correct type of demodulator can be selected.

On some sets there may be the option to switch in a beat frequency oscillator (BFO) so that Morse and SSB signals can be received. In these cases the position with the BFO out of circuit is used for AM reception. Also 'world band' receivers with a VHF / FM broadcast band will automatically switch to FM for this band.

A little practice is needed to tune in single sideband signals (**Fig 8.1**),

Mode switches on a communications receiver.

but after the first few signals have been tuned in it quickly becomes second nature. First set the receiver to either upper sideband (USB) for amateur transmissions above 10MHz or lower sideband (LSB) for amateur transmissions below 10MHz. Then slowly tune the receiver until a single sideband signal is heard. Tune the set slowly until the signal is at the correct pitch, and it should then become intelligible. If it does not, then change from USB to LSB or vice versa. For receivers where there is a BFO but no position for USB or LSB, turn the BFO off and then tune in a single sideband signal for maximum strength. Turn the BFO on and adjust it to give the correct audio pitch and intelligibility. It will be found that the BFO can be tuned either side to give the correct pitch, but it will only be intelligible in one position. Once set, the pitch control can normally be left in position for the next signal.

## FILTER BANDWIDTH

Choosing the correct bandwidth for a particular type of transmission can be very important. Different types of transmission occupy different amounts of bandwidth. Accordingly it is necessary to use the required bandwidth filter for any given type of transmission as described later in this chapter. Often the filters may be labelled for the type of transmission they are intended to receive. This makes it easy to identify the correct filter bandwidth.

## AUDIO FILTER

Some receivers use what is called an audio filter. As the name suggests, this is a filter that is placed in the audio stages of the receiver. These filters generally have two uses. One with a relatively high bandwidth can be used for reception of SSB signals and provides a reduction in the high frequency 'monkey chatter' noise that results from off-channel signals. However, audio filters are more widely used to give a very narrow band filter

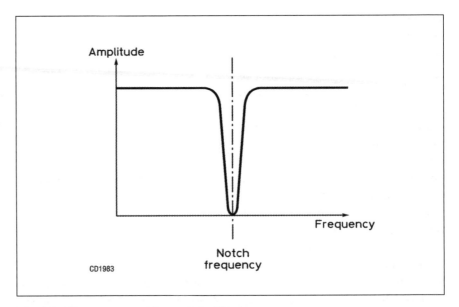

Fig 8.2. The response of a notch filter.

for use with Morse reception. When used with good filters in the previous stages of the receiver, audio filters can provide a very cost-effective method of gaining a very narrow bandwidth in the final stages of the set.

## NOTCH FILTER

When receiving SSB and Morse, annoying whistles or heterodynes may be present. These may be removed by a notch filter that may be adjusted in frequency and which removes a narrow band of frequencies, as shown in **Fig 8.2**.

## AGC

The strength of signals varies by an enormous amount. From the very weakest to the strongest the difference might be as much as 100 decibels (dB), ie a power ratio of 10,000,000,000 times. This is a vast range, and as a result receivers today have circuitry to adjust the level of gain in the set to accommodate this. The level of the signal is detected and a voltage is fed to the earlier stages so that the gain is reduced as the signals become stronger. The effect of this can be noted particularly well when receiving an AM station on a car radio.

As the car moves the signal level varies considerably but the output

level will remain almost constant. The main difference that is noticed is that as the signal becomes weaker the level of background noise or interference rises.

In some instances the AGC can be turned off, or the time constant associated with it can be changed. Generally a slow characteristic is required for SSB to enable the syllables of the speech to be accommodated. For Morse a faster AGC characteristic can be tolerated. In many cases, though, an option is not provided and the design of the receiver is optimised for all types of transmission.

## PRESELECTOR / RF TUNING

Although not particularly common these days, a preselector or RF tuning control may be found on some receivers. Its purpose is to adjust the tuning of the early stage or stages in the receiver so that they are exactly on tune. This is required because loading effects of the antenna, or the way in which they track or follow the tuning of the later stages may vary slightly.

By using this control the wanted signal level can be peaked and any unwanted signals arising from spurious responses in the receiver can be minimised.

## TYPES OF RECEIVER

The primary function of a receiver is to accept incoming signals, select the one on the required frequency, amplify it and then separate the modulation so that the signal can be heard via headphones or loudspeaker, or connected to another unit such as a computer for processing. However, there is a number of ways in which this can be achieved and there are several different types of receiver. The simplest is a *crystal set* consisting simply of a tuned circuit and diode detector or demodulator. These were some of the first receivers that were used, and they can still be built today.

*Tuned radio frequency (TRF)* receivers were also widely used - they included an amplifier to increase the signal strength. However, both of these sets lack the selectivity required on today's crowded bands. As a result two other types of receiver are more commonly used. These are the direct conversion receiver and the superhet.

## DIRECT CONVERSION

The *direct conversion* receiver is popular, especially with home constructors. It combines a high level of performance with a relatively straightforward and simple level of construction, although there are a couple of drawbacks that make it unsuitable for general use.

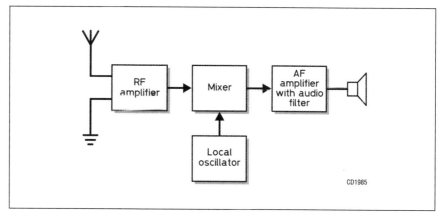

Fig 8.4. Block diagram of a direct conversion receiver.

One of the key processes that take place in the direct conversion receiver, and for that matter the superhet, is a process known as mixing. This is not the same as audio mixing, where two or more audio signals are summed to pass through an amplifier in the most linear fashion as possible to reduce distortion. Instead, radio frequency mixing is a *non-linear* process. Here the two inputs are *multiplied* together.

When this is done, a variety of signals are seen at the output. Not only are there the two original signals, but also two further signals at frequencies equal to the sum and difference of the input signals. In other words, if signals at 2MHz and 3MHz enter the mixer, new signals at 3MHz - 2MHz = 1MHz and 3MHz + 2MHz = 5MHz are seen, as shown in **Fig 8.3**.

The direct conversion receiver uses this process at the core of its operation. Signals enter the mixer from the antenna as shown in **Fig 8.4**. Here they are mixed with a locally-generated signal. If the local oscillator is running on a frequency of 1MHz and there is an incoming signal at 1.001MHz, signals at 0.001MHz or 1kHz and 2.001MHz will be produced. The signal at 2.001MHz is well above the audio range and will not pass through the filter and the audio amplifier. However, the signal at 1kHz will.

Tuning the receiver is then simply a matter of altering the frequency of the local oscillator. By tuning it up or down in frequency, different frequencies will mix with the oscillator and be allowed through the filter and into the audio amplifier. Sometimes radio frequency tuning ahead of the mixer is included. This is simply to prevent signals on all frequencies being presented to the mixer and overloading its input.

The problem with this type of receiver is that the signal being received will create what is known as a *beat note* with the local oscillator. This is fine for Morse signals as this will give the characteristic tone that is turned on and off. It also works well with single sideband. However, for AM it is necessary to tune the receiver so that it becomes 'zero beat' with the incoming signal, otherwise an annoying heterodyne or tone is heard. It is also not possible to receive FM with this type of receiver.

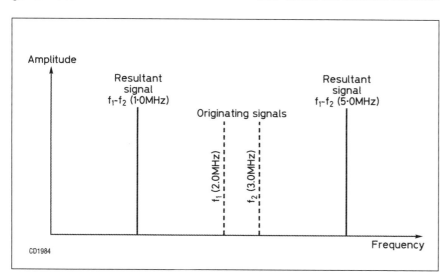

Fig 8.3. The mixing process.

A very high performance radio receiver. *(Image courtesy Icom UK)*

## SUPERHET

The superhet is by far the most common type of receiver in use today. From portable broadcast receivers to communications receivers, and hand-held walkie-talkies to mobile phones, the superhet is used in all of these applications and many more. It is more complicated than many other types of receiver such as the direct conversion, but it is far more versatile and capable of providing excellent results.

Like the direct conversion receiver the superhet uses the mixing process. However, this time the incoming signal is converted down to a fixed *intermediate frequency* (IF) stage where the signal is amplified. Once through this it is demodulated to regenerate the original audio signal.

A block diagram of a basic superhet radio is shown in **Fig 8.5**. Here it can be seen that the signal enters the RF amplifier. This stage not only provides some amplification

of the signal, but also some tuning. The signal enters the mixer and is mixed with a local oscillator signal. The output is then passed through the intermediate frequency (IF) amplifier and filter. It is in the IF stages where the main filtering occurs and stations on adjacent channels are rejected.

It is worth spending a little time looking more closely at the way in which this works. Take the example of a local oscillator running at a frequency of 5MHz. An incoming signal on 5.5MHz will mix with it to produce signals at 10.5MHz and 0.5MHz (ie 5.5 - 5.0MHz and 5.5 + 5.0MHz). If the IF is at a frequency of 0.5MHz the signal at 5.5MHz will be converted down to 0.5MHz and pass through the amplifier and filter. The signal at 10.5MHz will be ignored. By moving the local oscillator to 6.0MHz it can be seen that a signal at 6.5MHz will produce a signal at the output of the mixer and pass through the amplifier and filter.

The problem with the system is that it is possible for two signals to mix with the local oscillator and produce a signal at the intermediate frequency. With the local oscillator set to 5.0MHz we have seen that a signal at 5.5MHz will produce another signal at 0.5MHz after the mixer. However, it is also possible for a signal at 4.5MHz to mix with the local oscillator and give a signal at 0.5MHz. (5.0 - 4.5MHz gives a difference of 0.5MHz.) To prevent this signal from entering the mixer, tuning is incorporated in the radio frequency (RF) amplifier (see **Fig 8.6**). This tuning does not have to be very sharp because it is only required to remove the unwanted or image signal.

Once the signal has passed through the IF stages it needs to be demodulated. Different types of demodulator are usually required for different types of modulation. For amplitude modulation a simple *envelope detector* normally consisting of a diode and a few other components is needed. This senses the changes in the amplitude of the signal and converts them into voltage variations that can then be amplified and passed into the audio amplifier before being converted into sound waves by a loudspeaker or headphones. For single sideband and Morse a BFO and mixer is required. Often the mixer is referred to as a product detector in this application.

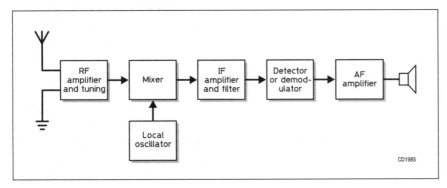

**Fig 8.5. Block diagram of a basic superheterodyne radio.**

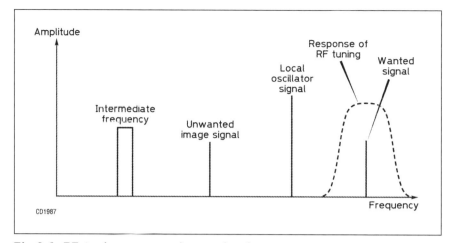

Fig 8.6. RF tuning removes image signals.

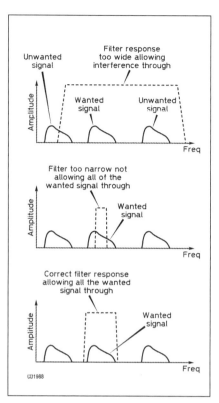

Fig 8.7. Selecting the correct filter bandwidth.

## SENSITIVITY

If a receiver is to be able to hear weak signals it must be as sensitive as possible. The actual sensitivity is not limited by the amount of gain that can be achieved. It is possible to obtain very high levels of gain with comparatively little difficulty. Instead the main limiting factor is noise. The receiver may pick this up from the antenna, or it may be generated within the set itself.

The received noise arises from a number of sources. It may be atmospheric noise from sources like thunderstorms or it may be galactic, coming from outer space. As the frequencies increase the received noise reduces and eventually a point is reached where the noise generated within the receiver circuitry dominates. As a very broad rule, it is found that on the short-wave bands the received noise dominates, but at VHF and above the noise generated within the receiver becomes the dominant factor.

For receivers on the short-wave bands a measure known as the *signal-to-noise ratio* is generally used. This looks at the level of input signal required to give a signal output compared to the noise output. Normally the signal-to-noise ratio is expressed in decibels (a method of comparing signals on a logarithmic basis). Typically a good short-wave communications receiver might have a sensitivity of 0.25µV for a 10dB signal-to-noise ratio in a 3kHz bandwidth using SSB. The lower the input voltage required to give the 10dB signal-to-noise ratio, the more sensitive it is.

For receivers that cover frequencies above 30MHz it is often more normal to quote a specification called a noise figure. This is a measure of how much noise a receiver or other item adds. A perfect unit would add no noise at all but this is obviously not possible.

The figure is expressed in decibels. For example, many preamplifiers have a noise figure of 1dB or better. A good receiver might have a noise figure of 4dB or more. General-coverage receivers might easily have a noise figure of 8 to 10dB. The lower the figure, the better the noise performance.

## SELECTIVITY

It is important to ensure that a receiver is able to remove or reject stations on adjacent channels sufficiently well. It is also important to have a variety of different degrees of selectivity in a good receiver because different modes of transmission occupy varying degrees of bandwidth. Accordingly it is important to match the receiver bandwidth to that of the mode of transmission being received. Too wide and the receiver will allow unwanted noise and interference through. Too narrow and the receiver

filters will not allow the whole of the transmission through, and this will result in distortion and loss of intelligibility.

Typically for an AM broadcast transmission a bandwidth of 6kHz is considered adequate for the short-wave bands. Around 9kHz may be used for the medium- and long-wave bands where better fidelity is required. For single sideband a figure of 2.5 or 3kHz is generally used and for Morse bandwidths of 500Hz, 250Hz or possibly less can be used, especially when conditions are difficult.

When specifying filters a variety of figures are used. With an ideal filter the *pass band*, the frequency band where signals are allowed through, and the *stop band*, the bandwidth for which signals are rejected, is the same. In reality it is not possible to make a perfect filter, although the performance of many filters, and especially crystal filters, is very good. The pass band is defined as the bandwidth where the signal drops by 6dB. The stop band

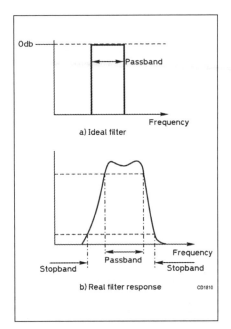

**Fig 8.8. Ideal and real filters.**

is the bandwidth where the signal level has dropped by 60dB as shown in **Fig 8.8**. In some instances the attenuation figures may vary, so it is usual for specifications to be in the form: a bandwidth of 2.7kHz at -6dB and 6kHz at -60dB.

## MODES REQUIRED

It is important to ensure that the receiver can accommodate the modes that are most likely to be received. In general a receiver for use on the short-wave bands should be able to resolve AM, SSB and Morse (CW). FM is used considerably less on these frequencies, and is really only used for CB and for some amateur transmissions at the top of the 10m band. On frequencies above 30MHz, narrow-band frequency modulation (NBFM) is more widely used, although in the aircraft band above 108MHz amplitude modulation is still used. Also radio amateurs use modes such as SSB and Morse, apart from the variety of data modes.

## BUYING A RECEIVER

A receiver will be one of the most expensive and important purchases for the station. Accordingly it is worth spending a little time to make sure that any receiver that is chosen will be suitable for what is required.

One of the first activities is to decide exactly what is wanted. Whilst this may sound a very obvious step, many people only have a vague idea of what they want when they start to buy a set. Especially if it is your first set, it is worth trying to borrow a receiver from a friend to get a feel for what you want. There is no point in spending plenty of hard-earned cash on a receiver only to find that it does not fit the bill after a short while. It is worth considering what type of listening is to be undertaken: short waves only; radio hams or general coverage; scanning VHF and UHF frequencies. It is also worth considering the facilities and general performance that are required. Price is also another important consideration and linked to this is the decision about buying new or second-hand.

When buying new first check out all the possible sets that are available. If possible get hold of data sheets to narrow down the choice. When a decision has been made, visit the dealer's show room and ask to use the receiver you are thinking of buying. If possible try to compare different receivers. Take some time to sit down with it and see whether it really meets the requirements. Does it have all the facilities required? Does it cover all the required bands? Finally, does it *feel* right and would you be happy with it?

It is also worth looking at the second-hand market. There are many good bargains to be had. A set can be bought from either a dealer or a private individual. Obviously a dealer has a reputation to maintain, and the receiver is likely to come with some form of guarantee. This adds to the cost, because nothing comes free and the dealer also has to make his profit and there will be VAT included in the sale.

Buying from private individuals can produce some excellent bargains, although there is a greater risk. If the person selling the equipment is known to you, so much the better. If not then a little more caution is needed. Many people who buy and sell cars look at the person selling it. The same idea can be used when buying radio equipment. For example if the house is well cared for then the same is likely to be true for the radio. Use these and other pointers to assess whether the person is likely to give you a good deal. If he is, that can give some degree of comfort. However, it is necessary to take a very good look at the receiver. It can help to take a friend along to give a second opinion and, if in doubt, don't buy the set.

Check the receiver over in a systematic fashion. Does it look as though it has been well cared for? Has it been extensively used? If so, items like switches may have become

A general-coverage communications receiver, suitable for listening on both the amateur bands and broadcast bands. *(Image courtesy Icom UK)*

worn. If it has been in a smoker's environment deposits may build up on switches, making them unreliable. Run though all the controls, checking that they operate correctly. Tune the receiver over all the bands. Can signals be heard at the right strength? Check the stability, especially on older receivers. Tune it into a broadcast station with the BFO switched on. By tuning the set to zero beat any drift should be quickly noticed. Another problem encountered on older sets is that the bandswitch may be very sensitive to any movement, giving a slight change in frequency if it is touched.

It is worth taking time - only make an offer when you feel perfectly happy that it is in good working order and that it is the receiver for you.

Whatever option you take up, a good receiver will provide many hours of pleasure. It is likely that it will still be very useful when transmitting on the air. Even though most transmitting stations use transceivers, a second receiver is always very handy.

## ADDITIONAL EQUIPMENT FOR RECEIVERS

Apart from the receiver itself there will be other items of ancillary equipment that can be used to improve the performance of the receiver or provide additional facilities.

One that many people use is an *antenna tuning unit (ATU)*. When connected correctly into the antenna system these units enable the best performance to be obtained from the antenna.

Other items can include *decoders* for the wide variety of data transmissions that can be heard on the bands these days. Most of the decoders are able to deal with a many types of transmission: Morse, packet, AmTOR, fax and so forth. However, before buying one check that it can decode all the

types of signal that you require now and for the future. A little time researching what is available can ensure the best buy is made.

For VHF and UHF, *preamplifiers* are available. They are most commonly seen for the 2m and 70cm amateur bands, where they can provide improved levels of sensitivity. However, *wide-band* preamplifiers are unlikely to give much improvement when used with most sets. They are in fact more likely to cause distortion that would give rise to the presence of unwanted spurious signals.

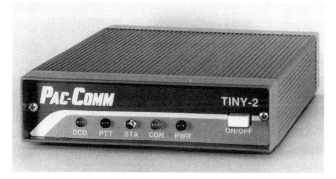

A digital modes adapter (TNC).

An antenna tuning unit.

### FURTHER INFORMATION
*Radio Communication Handbook*, 8th edn, Mike Dennison, G3XDV, and Chris Lorek, G4HCL (eds), RSGB, 2005.
*Superhet Radio Handbook*, Ian Poole, G3YWX, Bernard Babani (Publishing) Ltd.

# 9. Antennas

An HF Yagi beam antenna.

Photo:
9M6DXX

AN ANTENNA or aerial is an essential part of any radio station. Its performance will have a major influence on the operation of the entire station. A good antenna will make the most of the equipment, whereas a poor antenna will limit the performance of the equipment, however good it is. As a result time and energy invested in improving the antenna system is well spent. In fact experimenting with antennas is an enjoyable activity that can pay major dividends in terms of the performance of the whole station.

## WHAT IS AN ANTENNA?

An antenna is an element that picks up electromagnetic waves in the form of radio signals from the ether, enabling them to be passed into a receiver as high-frequency electrical signals. Conversely, when power from a transmitter is applied to an antenna this energy is converted into electromagnetic signals that are radiated.

This essentially makes the antenna the 'eyes' of the radio system. Using this analogy it is easy to imagine that the better placed the antenna system is, the better it will be able to 'see' or pick up the signals. Similarly, it will be able to transmit them better as well. Using another analogy, if a light is high up and has a better view of the surrounding area, the light can be seen more clearly further away. A well-placed antenna will be able to radiate its signal better if it is high up and in the open.

## AN ANTENNA SYSTEM

An antenna system consists of three main parts. The first is obviously the antenna element itself. The second is the feeder, and the third is the matching arrangement. The purpose of the antenna element has already been described: it is the part of the system that radiates or receives the electromagnetic signal.

However, the feeder is also very important. It enables the signal to be carried from the antenna to the receiver, or conversely from the transmitter up to the antenna. It is important that it introduces as little loss as possible because any loss in the feeder will degrade the performance of the whole system. As a result many people invest in expensive feeder to ensure that the minimum amount of power is lost.

Another requirement of a feeder is that it should not radiate or pick up signals. Not only will this incur power loss, but may also mean that inter-

ference is picked up if, for example, the feeder passes through a house where there could be plenty of interference generated. Also, when used with a transmitter, if power is radiated from the feeder it may cause interference to other users if it passes close to equipment that picks up the radiated signal.

Finally, there is the matching system, if required. Both feeders and antennas have an impedance. To ensure that the maximum amount of power is transferred from one to the other, both impedances must be matched. This may be achieved by using a matching unit. Often these may be referred to as an antenna tuning unit (ATU) or sometimes as an antenna matching unit (AMU).

## FEEDERS

There is a variety of types of feeder that can be used. Coaxial feeder ('coax') is the most widely used, whilst open wire or twin feeder is used

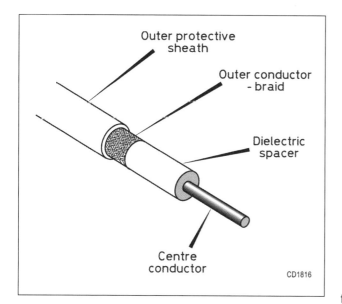

Fig 9.1. Coaxial feeder.

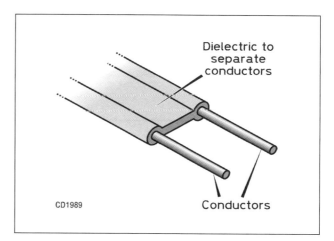

Fig 9.2. Twin feeder.

in some applications, especially for HF work.

Coaxial feeder consists of two concentric conductors. The inner conductor may be a single conductor or it may be made up of several strands. An insulating dielectric separates the two conductors. Usually this is a plastic material and is often in the form of foam, or it may have several tubes running along it. This is called semi-air spaced feeder and, being air spaced, it gives a lower level of loss. The outer conductor is normally in the form of a braid. Covering the braid there is an outer sheath. This provides protection for the feeder and prevents moisture ingress that would introduce loss.

Having a concentric construction means that the inner conductor is fully screened by the outer one and the signal being carried by the feeder is totally enclosed within the outer braid, so little of it escapes. It also means that the feeder is not affected by nearby objects and can easily be run through a house.

Most coaxial feeder has a characteristic impedance of either 50 or 75$\Omega$ (ohms). 75$\Omega$ feeder is used for domestic applications such as television and hi-fi radio, whereas 50$\Omega$ feeder is used for commercial applications, amateur radio and CB.

Open wire or twin feeder is used less frequently but nevertheless is still very useful. It consists of two conductors running parallel to each other. As the currents flowing in each of the wires are equal and opposite, the resulting fields around the wires cancel each other out and no signal is radiated.

Open wire feeder can be made in a number of ways. It is available commercially made but it is possible to make it yourself. The commercially made varieties come in two main forms but essentially consist of two wires spaced about 1.5cm apart with an insulating dielectric between them to keep the spacing constant (**Fig 9.2**).

There is the white opaque variety that is used, amongst other things, for making temporary VHF broadcast receiving antennas. This type of twin feeder is only suitable for internal use because the plastic absorbs moisture and when this occurs the losses rise.

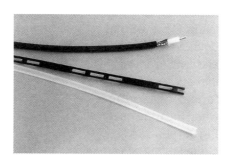

Coaxial cable, black twin and ordinary twin feeders.

However, there is another type. This uses a black plastic with holes cut in the spacing dielectric. Not only does having the holes in the dielectric spacing reduce the losses, but the plastic does not absorb water.

## POLARISATION

Light waves can be polarised and this can be illustrated very easily with a pair of Polaroid® sunglasses. Only when light is polarised in the right direction can the light pass through the Polaroid material. Radio waves can also be polarised and antennas will receive signals with a particular polarisation. A vertical antenna will receive vertically-polarised signals and similarly a horizontally-polarised antenna will receive horizontally-polarised signals. Where signals travel directly between one antenna and another it is important to ensure that the antenna polarisations are the same. If they are different, the signal levels will be reduced.

On the HF bands the antenna polarisation is not particularly critical. Once a signal has been reflected by the ionosphere it has both horizontally and vertically-polarised components. Accordingly it is possible to use an antenna with either polarisation, the main requirements being the type of antenna that best fits the location. At VHF and UHF vertically-polarised antennas are used universally for FM operation, with horizontal polarisation for DX work on SSB and Morse.

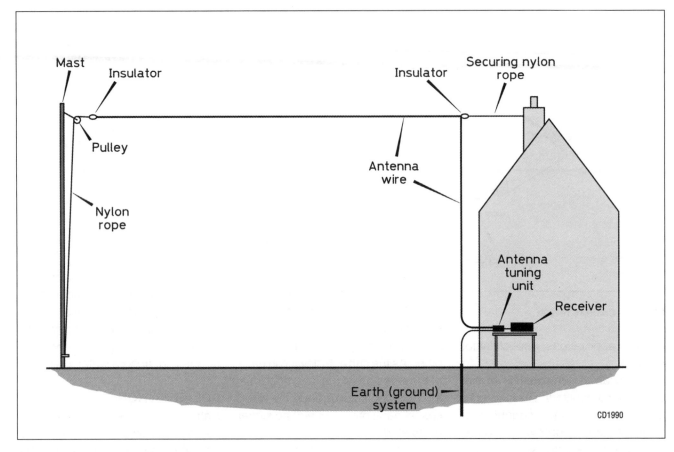

Fig 9.3. A typical end-fed wire installation.

## THE BASIC 'LONG WIRE' ANTENNA

One of the most popular antennas for receiving on the HF bands is often known as the 'long wire' antenna, although it should more exactly be called an 'end-fed wire' antenna. It is a very useful and versatile antenna and for receiving purposes it should be as reasonably long and as high as possible.

A long wire can be installed as shown in **Fig 9.3**, although almost any configuration can be used. It will be seen that insulators are used at the ends of the wire. These can be simple 'egg' insulators like those shown in the diagram. The full ribbed varieties are not really required. Polypropylene rope can be used to secure the insulators to the house and a suitable pole at the remote end. The down lead can then be brought into the shack.

A good earth is needed if a long wire is to be used successfully. Obviously, the mains earth can be used but this is likely to introduce high levels of noise. It is better to use a proper earth for the antenna as described later in the chapter.

Trees provide a convenient high structure that can be used to secure the remote end of an antenna. However, they do move in the wind and if this is not taken into account the antenna can suffer when the wind rises. **Fig 9.4** shows a simple system that can be used to overcome this problem. The

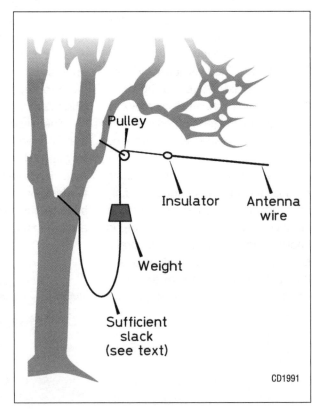

Fig 9.4. System for anchoring a wire antenna to a tree.

loop should contain sufficient slack to enable the full movement of the tree under the worst conditions but should not be so long that it becomes tangled easily.

Whilst long wires are very easy and convenient to install they have some disadvantages. They require the use of an ATU, especially if they are to be used for transmitting. They also radiate or pick up signals immediately they leave the ATU. This means that when they are used for transmitting there can be high levels of radio frequency power in the 'shack' or radio room which might be considered to be a health hazard if high powers are used. The high RF levels can also cause some equipment malfunctions. When used for receiving it means that the antenna is likely to pick up interference from domestic appliances, and the general noise level might be high when compared with other types of antenna that use coaxial or other types of feeder and are located away from the house.

## THE DIPOLE

The dipole is one of the most commonly used forms of antenna. It forms the basic element of a number of types of antenna, as well as being widely used in its own right. In its basic form it consists of a length of wire a half-wavelength long, cut in the middle to allow the feeder to be connected.

As the antenna must be a particular length, it only has a narrow bandwidth over which it can operate efficiently. Typically it will operate satisfactorily over a single amateur band but not very well outside it.

The actual length is slightly shorter than the half-wavelength in free space. The total length of the antenna can be determined quite easily from the formula:

Length (m) = 148 / Frequency (MHz)

Even though this is a relatively good guide to the length of the antenna it is always good practice to cut the wire slightly *longer* than is needed and then trim it to give the best performance. It is always easier to cut a little wire off than replace wire that has already been removed. A number of factors will affect the performance of the antenna, including the proximity of nearby objects.

Although a dipole is often thought of as a half-wave antenna, it is equally acceptable to have a dipole that is three, five or in fact any odd multiple of half-wavelengths long. This means that an antenna cut for operation on 7MHz can equally be used for operation on 21MHz. This makes the antenna useable on more than one band.

Using an antenna on more than one band can be achieved in other ways. One method is to cut several dipoles and run them from the same feeder, as shown in **Fig 9.6**. This system works quite well provided the wires are separated from one another reasonably well, and this limits the number to about three sets of wires. They also interact with one another slightly, so it is best to adjust the longest one first and then progress to the shortest.

| Frequency (MHz) | Length (metres) |
|---|---|
| 1.8 | 82 |
| 3.5 | 42 |
| 7.0 | 21 |
| 10.1 | 14.6 |
| 14.0 | 10.6 |
| 18.0 | 8.2 |
| 21.0 | 7.1 |
| 24.8 | 6.0 |
| 28.0 | 5.3 |
| 50 | 3.0 |
| 144 | 1.0 |
| 430 | 0.34 |

Table 9.1. Approximate lengths for half-wave dipole antennas.

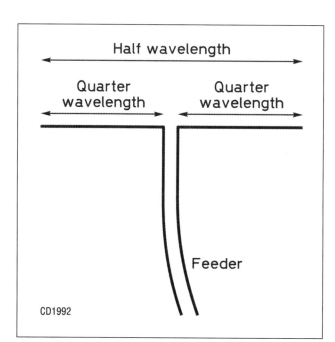

Fig 9.5. A dipole antenna.

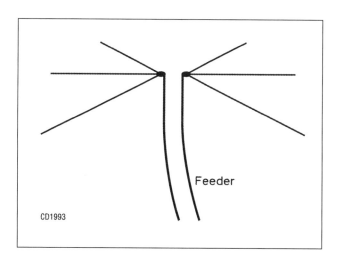

Fig 9.6. It is possible to run several dipoles from a single feeder.

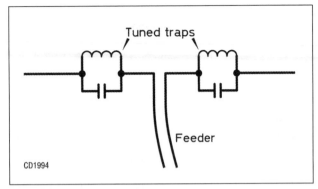

**Fig 9.7. A trap dipole.**

Another alternative is to place tuned circuits or (traps) in the antenna, as in **Fig 9.7**, so that at certain frequencies sections of it are isolated. When the antenna is operating at the resonant frequency of the trap, the latter acts as a high impedance and isolates the outer part of the antenna, thereby shortening it. When operated at another frequency the signal is able to pass through and the whole of the antenna is used. In this way the antenna has two resonant frequencies. It is possible to add further traps to increase the number of bands on which the antenna can operate.

## VERTICAL ANTENNAS

Horizontal antennas for the HF bands can take up a considerable amount of space, and not every garden is big enough. Vertical antennas can provide a solution in many respects, resulting in an efficient antenna in a small space. Most verticals are a quarter-wavelength long (high) and it is either possible to 'ground mount' them, or to use a set of radials (often four) as a ground plane against which the antenna can work. When ground mounted the antenna must be at ground level and a good earth connection must be provided for the antenna to work efficiently. When used with a ground plane the antenna can be operated well above ground, as the radials simulate the ground. There are generally four, and they are cut to be a quarter-wavelength on the frequency of operation.

In the same way that it is possible to have a trap dipole it is also possible to have a trap vertical. There is a wide variety of commercially made trap verticals. These normally cover a number of the HF bands and are made from aluminium tubing. Wider sections contain the traps for the different bands.

**A trap vertical antenna for the HF bands.**

Verticals are also widely used at VHF and UHF, especially on cars because they provide an 'all round' reception and transmission capability, enabling them to function regardless of the orientation of the car. Other antennas like dipoles are directive and would need to be rotated. When verticals are mounted on to cars, the car itself becomes the ground plane. Sometimes they are longer than a quarter-wavelength to give improved performance. For base stations, a quarter-wave ground plane with radials may be used but other designs that do not require a ground plane are more commonly used.

## BEAM ANTENNAS

To improve the performance of an antenna it is possible to beam the power in a particular direction. When transmitting this means that more power is directed where it is wanted and less is wasted by sending it off in directions where it is not needed. Similarly, when receiving these antennas are more sensitive in one direction than the others, reducing the reception of interfering stations.

There are several different types of beam but the most popular is called the Yagi, named after its inventor, a scientist from Japan. The main element in the antenna is the *driven element* (the dipole), to which the

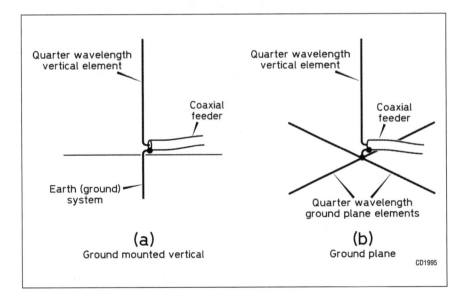

**Fig 9.8. The two main types of quarter-wave verticals: (a) ground mounted vertical, (b) ground plane antenna.**

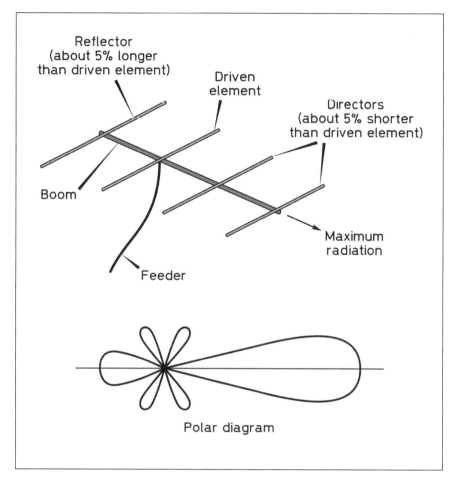

Fig 9.9. The Yagi beam antenna.

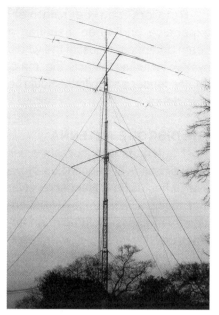

An HF antenna installation consisting of three Yagi beams.

feeder is connected. Behind the dipole is an element that is about 5% longer. This is known as the *reflector*, because it reflects signals back to the dipole. In front of the driven element there may be one or more elements that are about 5% shorter than the driven element. These are known as *directors*. Normally only one reflector is ever used, as adding additional reflectors beyond the first adds little to the performance. However, several directors are often used, each one improving the performance slightly. One of the most common uses for the Yagi is for television reception. These antennas have eight or more directors.

Radio amateurs use beams on a variety of frequencies. Some HF enthusiasts have arrays that cover three or more bands. Normally the lowest frequency they are used for is 14MHz, although a few beams are used on 7 and even 3.5MHz!

At VHF and above Yagis are widely used, especially for DXing. Antennas with eight or 11 elements are common, and for the serious operators antennas with more elements are employed to give the required levels of performance.

When using a directional antenna such as a Yagi, it is necessary to orientate it in the required direction. Normally this is achieved using a *rotator* that can be controlled from the same location as the receiver or transmitter. A motor on the antenna mast turns the antenna and will only rotate through 360° and then stop. It does not go round more than this to prevent the feeder becoming entangled. In the radio shack a controller sets the direction of the antenna, and naturally there is an interconnecting cable.

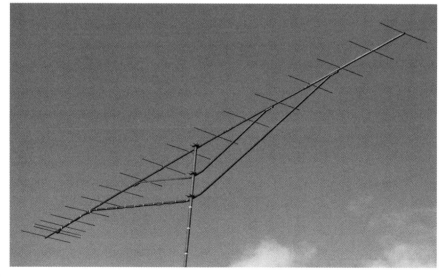

A Yagi antenna for one of the VHF bands.

Rotators can be relatively expensive and when installing a beam antenna the cost of the whole system including the antenna, mast, rotator, feeder and so forth should be considered.

## THE DISCONE ANTENNA

Most antennas only cover a small band or bands of frequencies. However, when using a scanner receiver that covers a wide range of frequencies it is necessary to have an antenna that covers a much wider range of frequencies than most antennas. There are a few wide-band antenna designs and of these the most popular type is called the *discone*. It gains its name from the fact that the elements of the antenna form a disc and a cone as shown in **Fig 9.10**. The discone may typically have a frequency range of up to 10:1, e.g. it might cover from 100MHz to 1000MHz, although many cover a much smaller range. This antenna is not generally used for transmitting as it is not as efficient as a fully resonant antenna.

## INSTALLATION

There is a number of aspects to be thought about when installing an antenna. It is obviously necessary to ensure that it operates optimally, and a little planning before it is erected will enable the choices to be made like the best site and the best way to install it. Ideally the antenna should be installed as high as possible. In this way it will have the best 'radio view' and it will be able to pick up and radiate signals better. The higher the antenna is placed will mean that the horizon will be further away and this will increase the ranges that can be achieved, especially at VHF and above. The antenna should also be kept away from objects that might shield it. It is essential to keep it as far away from any metallic objects as possible. This might include telephone wires and many other items. Trees can also have an effect particularly when they are wet.

It is also an advantage if the antenna can be kept away from the house. Not only can this act as a screen but it can also be a source of interference, especially on the lower frequencies.

Whilst this is a wish list, any antenna installation will be something of a compromise. Various requirements may have to be traded off against one another to achieve the best overall result. While it is very nice to have an external antenna this is not always possible. Not all is lost if an internal antenna has to be used. The loft or attic is usually the best place, but remember to keep the antenna as far away from the water tank as possible. Also bear in mind that, being inside the house, interference levels will be higher. Not only will this affect the receiver, but when transmitting there is a greater chance of interfering with domestic appliances. Also signal levels will be lower as a result of being inside.

## SAFETY

One major aspect that must be borne in mind when installing any antenna is that of safety. This is of paramount importance because injuries have resulted either when installing antennas, or if they have fallen down. At all times keep an eye open for any problems that might occur. Remember that once an antenna has been exposed to the weather for a while corrosion will occur. Only use the best components, and make sure they are installed correctly. Under no

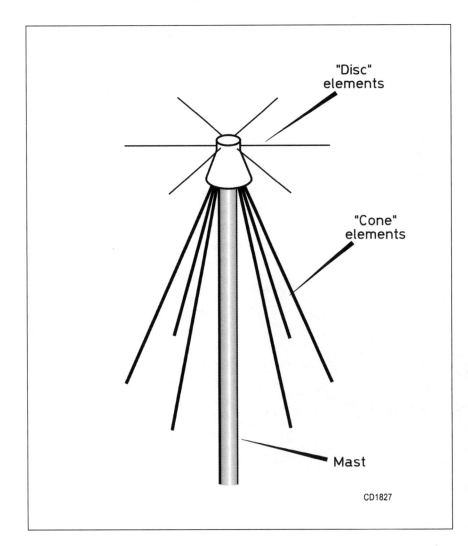

**Fig 9.10. A discone antenna.**

Photo: 9M6DXX

**Safety is of paramount concern when working on antennas. Always use a safety harness!**

circumstances should an antenna be liable to fall on to a power line.

Take great care when installing the antenna itself: people have been injured and even killed when installing antennas. Make sure that any ladders that are used are safe, and that you take precautions when working at any heights. Always make sure that a friend is there in case an accident occurs. This may sound alarmist, but accidents do occasionally occur. By taking precautions it is possible to minimise this possibility so that the hobby can be enjoyed without the worry of injuries.

## EARTH SYSTEM

An earth system is essential to the operation of many antennas including long (or end-fed) wires and ground-mounted verticals. The ground can conduct electricity, although its resistance is very high. However, as there is plenty of it the resistance between two areas can be very low. The problem is making a good contact to it. There are several ways in which this can be done. The easiest is to use an earth stake. This can be obtained from electrical wholesalers and suppliers and consists simply of a rod which is driven into the ground. To reduce the resistance further several can be connected in parallel. Alternatively lengths of copper pipe can be buried. Others have used old water tanks. It does not really matter.

Ideally the earth should be as close to the feed point of the antenna as possible. Many of the HF quarter-wave verticals state that the earth connection should be not more than 20 or 30cm from the antenna.

### FURTHER READING

*Backyard Antennas*, Peter Dodd, G3LDO, RSGB, 2000.
*HF Antennas for All Locations*, 2nd edn, Les Moxon, G6XN, RSGB, 1993.
*Radio Communication Handbook*, 8th edn, Mike Dennison, G3XDV, and Chris Lorek, G4HCL (eds), RSGB, 2005.
*Practical Wire Antennas 2*, Ian Poole, G3YWX (ed), RSGB, 2005.

# 10. Setting up the Station

A well-equipped radio shack.

**M**OST PEOPLE interested in amateur radio and short wave listening will want to set up their own station. At first this may only consist of a radio receiver which can be easily placed in a convenient corner. However, as interest grows it is likely that more equipment will be bought, wall maps may be put up and other items required. With this in mind it is convenient to set aside some space for a station or 'radio shack'.

The shack need not be a complete room, although this is what many people would like. There are many ways of setting aside some space for the radio equipment. A little ingenuity can enable areas of the house that were previously unused to be converted into quite luxurious shacks. To achieve this it is first necessary to look at some of the basic requirements, and then see what areas could be converted.

A variety of areas can be considered: spare rooms, loft spaces or attics, cupboards large and small, spaces in the garage, garden sheds and a whole host more. Each has its own advantages and disadvantages, and by applying a little thought it is often possible to make each one into a good home for the radio equipment.

## REQUIREMENTS

Before settling on the location of the shack it is worth considering the requirements. For example, some locations may not have easy access for antenna feeders, or mains power may have to be run in specially and these need to be taken into account. Additionally there must be sufficient space. Some shacks tend to grow quite quickly as more equipment is required and all the ancillary items such as components are acquired. On the other hand it may be possible to keep the amount of equipment to a minimum and utilise a much smaller space.

Other considerations include aspects such as noise. The noises emanating from a radio may not be quite as interesting or pleasing to others in the house, and this might mean that it is best to keep it out of the earshot of others by being able to shut a door on the noise. Similarly noises from the rest of the household may distract you from listening and result in you not being able to hear that weak and interesting DX station. It is also worth bearing in mind that you may not want the equipment accessible to others, especially if there are small children in the house.

Other aspects like warmth and convenience are also important. It is no fun operating a station when it is very cold or too hot. It takes away much of the real enjoyment and limits the times when the hobby can be enjoyed. The ease with which the station can be accessed may be an issue. It can be very nice to drop into the shack for five minutes to see what conditions are like, or leave the set on so that the bands can be monitored from time to time during the day.

There should also be sufficient room. It should obviously be possible to accommodate all the equipment, and other paraphernalia that is accumulated over the years. There should be sufficient room for a comfortable seat. The hobby is after all a relaxation and a comfortable seat is a definite advantage.

Finally, the table should be deep enough to hold the equipment with several centimetres behind to enable the cables and connectors to be accommodated, remembering that the coax used may not be very flexible. In addition to this there should be sufficient room in front of the equipment to rest your arm. This is particularly important if long periods of operating are envisaged. Typically this might mean that about 35 to 45cm space in front of the equipment is required.

## POSSIBILITIES

There are many places that can be considered. A spare room is obviously favourite, as it enables the equipment to be contained within one area, it can be shut off from the rest of the family and there should be sufficient space for the equipment. Mains power and access for the feeders should also not be a problem.

Unfortunately not all of us have this luxury and other options need to be considered. Sometimes this will require a compromise, but some excellent stations have been set up in very restricted spaces.

There are several ideas that can be investigated. The first is the loft or attic. In many houses there is a large amount of space in the loft and many people have set their stations there. One of the main disadvantages is that this area becomes very hot in summer and cold in winter. Also care must be taken to ensure that the timbers in the loft are not overloaded and that, if alterations need to be made, any building precautions are observed. It is always best to seek expert advice.

An external shed is another option. Whilst many garden sheds may be dirty and uninviting, a little work can convert these into very comfortable locations for a shack. Lining the walls and roof can help retain heat for the winter, and there is good access for feeders. Normally running mains power should not be a problem. The main drawback is security because a shed is reasonably easy to break into, and is not part of the main house. This could make it an easy target.

A garage is another consideration. Normally mains power is available, and feeder access may not be a problem. There may also be plenty of space. However, a garage may be cold in winter and other areas of it may impinge on the radio shack.

Some large walk-in cupboards offer a considerable amount of opportunity and can be made into a very attractive and inviting shack. Careful design is required to make the most of the space, and access for mains and feeders may require some work. However, being inside the house means that warmth and security should not be major issues.

Naturally these are not the only possibilities. There are many other areas around the house or flat that can be put to good use. A little thought, ingenuity and planning can make a good shack of many unlikely areas.

## LIGHTING AND WIRING

When planning and constructing the shack, care should be taken in planning both the mains wiring and the lighting. As far as the mains wiring is concerned, it is necessary to install sufficient sockets to supply the equipment that is currently in use as well as allowing some expansion for the future. The multi-way mains connector blocks that are available in DIY stores provide an ideal solution and can be mounted under the back of the table. In this way cables can be routed neatly out of the way. However, it is necessary to remember to allow sufficient space behind the table surface to enable cables with their connectors to be passed up and down. If there is insufficient space the connector may have to be removed from the cable to pass it down to the mains socket, when it must

then be reconnected.

Lighting is another important issue. The table surface should be well illuminated if the most is to be made of the shack. If one light source is provided from the middle of the room, the table surface will always be in the shadow of the person using the equipment. This will be a particular problem if any construction work is undertaken. The ideal solution is to have an angle poise lamp that can be used to illuminate the work area in addition to the main room lighting. Alternatively a small strip lamp can be placed under a shelf over the table surface, although a shade will be required to ensure that it does not shine directly in the user's eyes. Also remember to adhere to the manufacturer's fitting instructions.

## EQUIPMENT LIST

A variety of items will be needed for the shack. Obviously the items needed will depend upon what is already available and the plans for the station. However the shopping list below is a good starting point for a basic transmitting station:

- HF transceiver (or separate transmitter and receiver)
- Power supply for the transceiver (if one is not supplied). Make sure it can supply sufficient current for the transceiver.
- VSWR meter (if one is not already included in the transceiver)
- Ferrite rings for interference suppression (see below)
- Antenna tuning unit (ATU)
- Patch cables to connect the transceiver to the VSWR meter and

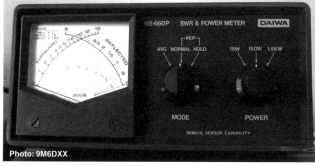
Photo: 9M6DXX

A useful piece on ancillary equipment: a VSWR meter.

then the ATU (remember to buy the right connectors for each connection)
- Microphone (remember that the correct connector will be needed for the particular transceiver being used, as the type of connector or wiring varies from one manufacturer to another)
- Morse key (again remember the connector)
- Loudspeaker and / or headphones (again check on the connector required for the loudspeaker). Note that often a loudspeaker is contained within the transceiver.
- Antenna (don't forget the connector to connect the feeder to the ATU)
- Logbook, scrap paper for notes and a pen
- Clock
- Prefix list
- World map.

If the station is to only be used for receiving, items such as the ferrite rings, VSWR meter, microphone, and Morse key will not be needed.

## CONNECTING UP THE STATION

There are many ways in which the equipment in an amateur radio station can be connected up. To an extent it will depend upon the equipment being used, but there are some basic guidelines that can be followed whatever the set-up and whatever is available. Unfortunately the electrical connections may not always fit in with the most ergonomic use of the equipment, but wires are flexible and can often be made to length, and it is necessary to connect the equipment in the correct way to ensure that the best performance is obtained.

A basic diagram for the way in which a basic station must be connected is shown in **Fig 10.1**. Basically, the power supply for the transceiver is connected to the power source, typically the mains. The power supply is connected to the transceiver which in turn is connected to a VSWR meter. This measures the actual VSWR being seen by the transceiver. This is very important be-

cause transistor output stages do not like high levels of VSWR. While it is useful to reduce the VSWR between the ATU and the antenna, the crucial area is to reduce the VSWR seen by the transceiver output.

The other point

Clip-on ferrites.

which will be seen from the diagram is that ferrite rings are used around the leads to and from the power supply. These reduce the level of RF leaking into the mains supply which can cause interference to other items of mains-powered electronics equipment such as hi-fi sets and televisions. If power supply leads have moulded-on plugs, it is possible to use a clip-on ferrite as an acceptable alternative. This does not, however, remove the need for a good RF earth such as a copper pipe driven well into the ground.

## EQUIPMENT AND LAYOUT

The layout of the equipment on the table is particularly important if the station is to be used for long periods of time, such as occurs if involved in contests, for example.

It is best to have the main transceiver or receiver in the centre of the table. This makes it easy to rest one's arm on the table and operate the tuning control, resulting in far easier operation over long periods of time. Other large pieces of

equipment can be placed either side. A linear amplifier or second receiver could easily be placed here. The microphone can be positioned on the left-hand side, leaving the right side free for writing and taking notes. Similarly the Morse key, if used, can be positioned on the right-hand side of the table (obviously these positions can be reversed for left-handed operators!)

There should also be sufficient space on the table for a log book and notepad; very useful for making notes whilst the other station is transmitting, or for copying down Morse.

A shelf above the main equipment is often very useful. This can hold ancillary equipment such as a VSWR meter, antenna tuning unit, clock and so forth.

Thought should also be given so that a computer can be conveniently located in the station if one is required. Sufficient space should be given to be able to locate it conveniently, bearing in mind that modern screens are large and deep. It is necessary to leave sufficient room

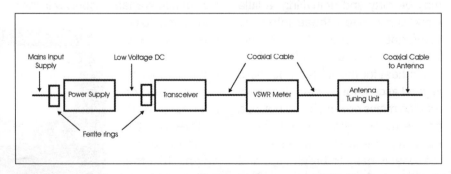

Fig 10.1. **Connecting equipment in an HF amateur radio transmitting station.**

for the keyboard and to rest your arms when typing.

Also, for those who enjoy construction, a separate area or work surface slightly away from the main station can be an advantage.

A pin board can be mounted on the wall. This can be used for a map. Dependent upon the bands in use and the likely ranges contemplated, the map could be a world map or one covering possibly your own country or continent. QSL cards and awards can also be mounted. Many QSL cards are very colourful and can add interest to the station. Awards are also worth displaying. Often people use proper picture frames for the awards as they will have spent time working towards them. Many people may not want to put pins through the cards. This can be avoided by mounting the QSL cards on to backing cards using photo corners.

## SAFETY

A major consideration in any station is that of safety. It is obviously im-possible to describe all the features that should be employed here, but we will just give a flavour of some of the points that might be noted.

It is worth using a residual current circuit breaker (RCCB) in the mains circuit for the shack. Although these breakers are not a substitute for other safety measures, they are able to provide an additional level of protection against electric shock.

Obviously all the mains wiring should be carefully done, observing the required regulations. Do not be tempted to leave earth connections off or take other short-cuts. It should be remembered that others, including children, may enter the shack and may not be aware of the potential dangers. In fact it is best to make the shack as child-proof as possible if there is any chance of them entering.

Other precautions include making sure that no hazardous voltages are accessible. Soldering irons should always be kept in a holder, and switched off when others are around and when they are not in use.

Overall the main action is to have a general awareness of safety. It is unlikely that an accident will occur, but the small chance can be reduced to the absolute minimum by making sure all the safety precautions are observed and any potential hazards are minimised. In this way the hobby can be enjoyed in a relaxing fashion, knowing that you and any visitors that may enter the shack will not come to any harm.

**FURTHER READING**
*The RSGB Amateur Radio Operating Manual*, 6th edn, Don Field, G3XTT (ed), RSGB, 2004.
*Radio Communication Handbook*, 8th edn, Mike Dennison, G3XDV, and Chris Lorek, G4HCL (eds), RSGB, 2005.

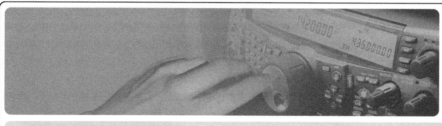

# 11. Constructing Your Own Equipment

THERE IS AN enormous sense of achievement when a piece of equipment you have built yourself works. This is particularly true when a new homebuilt transmitter is first put on the air and a station comes back to a call. Then with great pride you can say that *you* built it.

Today the need for home construction is much less than it used to be. In the very early days of amateur radio there was no commercially made equipment but in recent years virtually everything that is needed can be bought ready built. Combined with the greater availability, it is also becoming more difficult for homebuilt equipment to compete in terms of price and performance with the highly sophisticated equipment that can be bought from the amateur radio dealers or on the second-hand market.

Yet despite this many people enjoy building their own equipment. Most of it does not have nearly the same complexity and the same number of facilities as that which can be bought, but it is still possible to use it and gain some very good results. In fact some people take pride in the fact that they use *only* homebuilt equipment and they manage to obtain some excellent results from it. It brings a new dimension to the hobby.

## OPTIONS AVAILABLE

Several options are open to people wanting to build equipment. The first step is to choose a project that you have a good chance of completing: many people start projects that are never completed. Actually completing gives a tremendous sense of achievement and an incentive to start another item that may be slightly more advanced.

The equipment need not be a transmitter or receiver, it could be a piece of ancillary equipment - possibly an antenna tuning unit (ATU). However, simple Morse transmitters can be quite easy to put together and can be fun to set up and test.

The project can be undertaken in a number of ways. Possibly the easiest and most attractive option for many is to build a kit. There are several companies that advertise a good selection of kits for everything from an antenna tuning unit up to transmitters and receivers. In many cases the metalwork can also be bought, enabling the whole job to have a very professional looking finish.

The amateur radio and electronics magazines also publish a number of projects. These are normally more challenging because the whole project has to be assembled from scratch, assuming a kit is not available. However, they can provide some very good experience, although be careful not to start with a project that is too large or complex.

## EQUIPMENT

In any amateur radio station, be it for listening or transmitting, a certain number of tools will be required. A good selection of screwdrivers, spanners and the like are very useful. In addition to this a good pair of thin-

*A typical CW transmitter kit.*

Photo courtesy of Walford Electronics

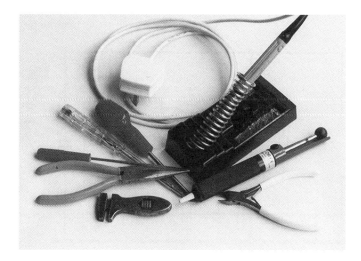

A selection of tools.

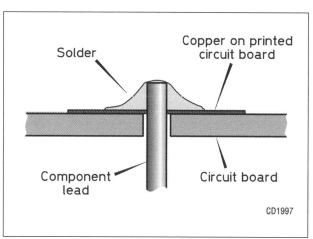

Fig 11.1. A soldered joint on a printed circuit board showing the amount of solder that should be used.

nosed pliers and wire cutters are essential. It is worth buying reasonable-quality tools. The very cheap ones will not last as long and may damage the screws, nut and bolts etc, causing more work.

A soldering iron is also needed. Even if little construction is envisaged, one will come in useful for making interconnection leads and setting up and keeping the station running.

Generally a 15-watt iron is suitable for most applications, although for items that are larger and absorb more heat a 25-watt iron comes in useful. Normally it is not necessary to spend a lot of money on a soldering iron, but if a really good item is required the thermostatically controlled versions are very nice. Most irons these days come with a stand. This is almost essential because the tips become very hot and will cause a burn if touched.

Another useful item for any-one contemplating using a soldering iron is a solder sucker. This can be used to remove the solder from joints and is almost essential when dismantling something or remaking a joint. Although it is possible to survive without one, it is an extremely useful item to have and can make some jobs very much easier.

## SOLDERING

Soldering is at the very heart of electronic construction and whether used for amateur radio construction or in professional electronic equipment it is equally important. Fortunately it is a skill that is learned relatively easily. One of the main requirements is that the job should not be rushed and it should be done carefully. Then with a little practice the standard of construction can be very high.

When making a joint, the first requirement is that both surfaces should be clean and free from any

oxidation. The iron should be at its operating temperature and the bit should be 'tinned', ie it should have a thin layer of solder applied to it. Both wires or surfaces should also be tinned so they can be soldered more easily. This will help remove any grease and dirt so that a good joint can be made. In fact, most leaded components are pre-tinned to help in the soldering process and if so tinning may not be required.

Both surfaces to be soldered should be brought together. This may entail mounting a component on a printed circuit board, twisting two

A neatly constructed piece of equipment.

wires together or possibly inserting wires into a connector for assembly. Once this is done the iron should be brought to the joint, and solder applied to the joint itself. Note that the solder should not be applied to the soldering iron first.

The best joints are made if they are done reasonably quickly. If the solder is kept very hot by the iron for too long the flux will be used up, allowing oxidation. This will lead to what is known as a *dry joint*. These look frosted and do not have the shiny appearance of a good joint. Dry joints can be very troublesome, giving a poor connection that may be intermittent.

The amount of solder used to make a joint should be carefully regulated. Enough should be used for it to flow round the joint, but it should not form a large blob over it. With a little practice it soon becomes obvious how much to use.

After the iron has been used for a few joints it will become blackened with the spent flux. This should be removed periodically by wiping the bit on a small damp sponge or cloth. These are normally supplied with the soldering iron stand and should be dampened from time to time. Keeping the bit clean will help to ensure that the solder flows easily over the soldering iron and that good joints are made.

A well-constructed piece of equipment can look very pleasing when complete. A well thought out project that has been carefully made is far more likely to work than one that has been quickly put together. It will also give more pleasure and can be shown to others with pride.

## BEAT FREQUENCY OSCILLATOR (BFO) PROJECT

Many domestic receivers can receive signals on the short-wave bands. However, many do not have a beat frequency oscillator (BFO) and as a result they cannot properly resolve Morse code or single sideband (SSB)

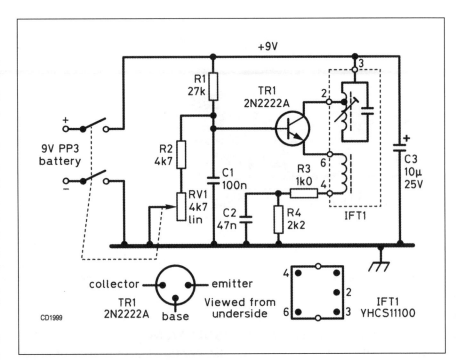

**Fig 11.2. Circuit diagram of the BFO project.**

signals. Fortunately it is relatively easy to build a small BFO using a handful of components.

This project will work with receivers having an intermediate frequency (IF) of between 450 and 470kHz. This IF is used by most receivers. The BFO can sit close to the receiver and does not require any direct connections for it to operate satisfactorily, making it an ideal first project.

The BFO can be made on a small piece of matrix board. This is board with a matrix of holes normally spaced 0.1in apart. Components can be mounted on the board with their leads routed through the holes to keep them in place. Alternatively, special pins can be mounted into the holes and components soldered to them. Once built, the BFO can be housed in a plastic box to protect the circuitry and keep it looking tidy. A metal box cannot be used, because this would screen the signal from the radio and prevent the BFO from working.

The circuit diagram is shown in **Fig 11.2**. From this it can be seen that it uses a single transistor and a few other components. A layout is

shown in **Fig 11.3**. However, before installing the transformer IFT1 the metal can should be removed to expose the transformer itself. This will help the signal to radiate and be picked up by the receiver a short distance away. Once this is done the components can be installed and carefully soldered, making sure that each joint is satisfactory. Underneath the board the components can be linked using connecting wire. This should be insulated wire, and each end can be stripped to leave a short length of conductor for soldering. Care should be taken not to leave the soldering iron too long on any of the components, especially the transistor, as otherwise damage may result. Also, make sure that C3 is connected the right way round, and that the connections of the transistor are correct.

The leads to the variable resistor/switch (RV1) and the 9V battery should be about 10cm long. Connect these before fitting RV1 into the case so that the circuit can be adjusted before fitting it into the case.

Once a final check has been done to ensure that all the components have been connected

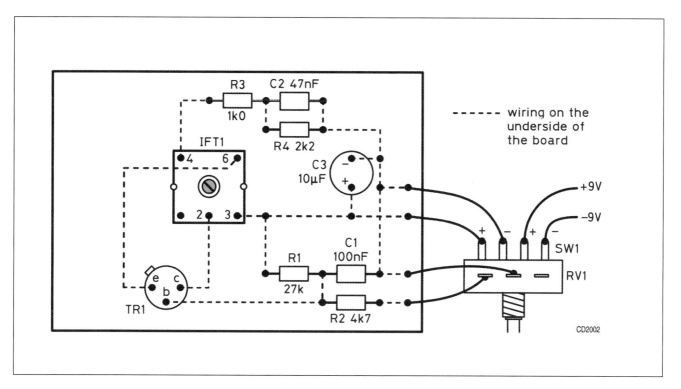

Fig 11.3. Matrix board layout and wiring for the BFO.

correctly and that all the wiring is correct, connect the battery. The assembly should be placed close to the radio it is to be used with. The radio should be set to an amateur band and then carefully tuned until a single sideband signal is heard. Then turn on the BFO and set the variable resistor to the mid position. Slowly adjust the ferrite core with a small screwdriver, or better still a plastic trimmer tool. Be careful with the core because it is fragile and can easily break. The ferrite core should be adjusted until the SSB speech starts to become intelligible. Once set to the optimum position, the core should be left and any further adjustments made with the potentiometer.

With the BFO working, it is worth experimenting with the best position for it. The assembly can be mounted in the plastic box. A 10.5mm hole can be drilled for the potentiometer RV1 and the matrix board can be mounted on pillars to secure it neatly. Finally, screw the base on the box and the unit is completely ready for use. However, remember to turn the BFO off when the radio is turned off.

| R1 | 27k 0.25 watt resistor |
| R2 | 4k7 0.25 watt resistor |
| R3 | 1k 0.25 watt resistor |
| R4 | 2k2 0.25 watt resistor |
| RV1 | 4k7 linear variable resistor (potentiometer) with switch |
| | |
| C1 | 100nF ceramic capacitor |
| C2 | 47nF ceramic capacitor |
| C3 | 10uF electrolytic capacitor (radial type) |
| TR1 | 2N2222A transistor |
| IFT1 | Toko YHCS11100 intermediate frequency transformer |
| | |
| Plastic box | Approx 100 x 70 x 45mm |
| Matrix board | Approx 80 x 50 mm (to fit box) |
| Battery connector | For PP3 |
| Control knob | To fit potentiometer spindle |

Table 11.1. Components list for the BFO project.

**FURTHER READING:**
*Practical Projects*, George Brown, M5ACN, RSGB, 2002.
*Circuit Overload*, John Fielding, ZS5JF, RSGB, 2006.
*RF Design Basics*, John Fielding, ZS5JF, RSGB, 2007.
*Electronics and Radio Today* website:
www.electronics-radio.com/articles/constructional_techniques/index.php
(information and advice on construction, soldering etc).

# 12. Getting Your Own Licence

ONCE YOU HAVE spent time listening on the bands, the next stage is to gain a transmitting licence. This opens a whole new field of amateur radio, enabling you to make friends all over the world, experiment with equipment, install your own transmitting station and fully participate in the hobby in whatever way you want.

To do this it is necessary to obtain an amateur transmitting licence. However, international regulations requires countries not to issue licences without the applicants proving that they are able to install, maintain and operate their equipment properly. Someone who did not have the relevant knowledge could cause considerable amounts of interference to others world-wide. Fortunately it is not difficult to obtain a licence, and gaining one gives a real feeling of achievement, apart from the fact that you will know more about radio and its technology.

Different countries have different requirements but international agreements lay down some basic requirements. There used to be a requirement for those with access to the HF bands below 30MHz to have to pass a Morse code test. This requirement no longer exists, and many countries including the UK do not require holders of these licences to take a Morse test. Instead different levels of theory and practical tests are required.

## UK LICENCES

In the UK there are three classes of licence that can be obtained. Each one gives a different level of privileges and requires tests at a different level to be passed. The licences are:

*1. Foundation licence*
*2. Intermediate licence*
*3. Full (or Advanced) licence*

Newcomers have to start by gaining a Foundation licence which provides an easy way to start transmitting, but it offers the least privileges. The next stage is to move on to the Intermediate licence which offers more frequency bands, modes and higher power levels. Finally it is possible to gain the Full licence which allows access to all the UK frequency allocations, the greatest flexibility and the highest powers. Each licence level has to be achieved before the next can be taken. This has to be done because the training and tests are structured so that additional privi-

Photo: Felixstowe & DARS

Foundation licence course students from Kesgrave School, Ipswich (and their teacher!) learn about antennas from members of the Felixstowe and District ARS.

leges are given as the level of training and experience increases.

## FOUNDATION LICENCE

The entry level amateur radio licence is the Foundation licence which was introduced in January 2002. The Foundation licence has been designed to get people on the air as quickly as possible. However, as it is possible to cause interference to other users, both within and outside the amateur bands, it is necessary to know something of how radios work and the ways of preventing interference. It is also necessary to know about the licence regulations.

In order to be able to obtain a Foundation licence it is necessary to attend a Foundation Licence Training Course. These are organised on behalf of the RSGB, and they must be successfully completed before a licence can be issued. Most of the training during the course is of a practical nature. There is a small amount of radio and electronics theory but this is aimed at providing an understanding for many of the practical issues, eg providing an appreciation of the correct fuses to use in equipment or how to construct an antenna or how to gain the best performance from a radio station.

While the thought of a training course may seem daunting at first, they are run in an informal and friendly manner by experienced and enthusiastic radio amateurs. They are normally run at a local amateur radio club, or for younger participants they may be run at a local school. They are usually run over a weekend. The course normally takes between 10 and 12 hours to complete. At the end, after all the practical elements have been completed, there is a short examination comprised of 25 multiple choice questions. The exam paper is marked at the time and if successful a pass certificate is given.

Once the pass certificate has been gained, it is possible to apply for a Foundation licence. Callsigns are

Photo: Keighley College STAR Centre

Air Cadets from 44F Squadron Bradford celebrate with their tutor (fourth from left) after all six passed the Foundation exam.

in the series M3***, with regional variations for Wales, Scotland, Northern Ireland etc. These licences allow access to the amateur allocations from 135.7kHz up to 70cm (430 - 440MHz) and there is also one at10 GHz. There is generally a power limit of 10 watts output, except for the 135.7 - 137.8kHz band, which is limited to 1 watt ERP (effective radiated power) for all licence classes; 431 to 432MHz where Foundation licensees are limited to 10 watts ERP; and 10GHz, where the power limit is 1 watt.

Although this may be thought of as low power it is still sufficient to allow communications around the world on the HF bands and good distances at frequencies above this. Even many radio amateurs with full licences, which allow them to use much higher power levels, prefer to operate at low power.

## INTERMEDIATE LICENCE

Once the Foundation licence has been gained, it is possible to look towards working for the next level, which is the Intermediate licence. To obtain the Intermediate licence it is advisable, although not mandatory, to take a training course. This course is longer than the Foundation licence course and it aims to teach many of the fundamentals of radio. The course has been planned to present the information in a stimulating way by actually

undertaking practical tasks such as soldering, building a small project and a variety of other exercises. This builds on the experience that will have been gained as a Foundation licence holder. There is also a need to have practical elements completed and assessed.

After completing the course and practical exercises, candidates sit the Intermediate licence examination. Again this examination is a multiple-choice test based on what was learnt on the course. It covers the basic concepts of radio operating on the amateur bands and the licence conditions. With both of these successfully completed an Intermediate licence can be obtained.

The Intermediate licence allows more privileges on the amateur bands. It allows access to all the amateur radio bands (HF / short wave, VHF / UHF and Microwaves). The maximum power level is also greater than that allowed for the Foundation licence and is generally 50 Watts, except for the 135.7 - 137.8kHz band, which again is limited to 1 watt ERP; 1.850 to 2.000MHz, where it is 32 watts; and 431 to 432MHz where it is 40 watts ERP.

Callsigns for the Intermediate Licence are issued in the series 2*. The country variants of 2E for England, 2I for Northern Ireland, 2M for Scotland, 2W for Wales etc are used, dependent upon the location within the UK that the station is located.

## FULL LICENCE

The Full licence, as the name suggests, is the licence which allows the most privileges, but it requires the Advanced Radio Communications Examination to be taken and passed. This syllabus is set at a higher level than that for the Intermediate licence. Again it covers radio theory and licence conditions but, because holding a Full licence enables the use of higher power levels, subjects including Electro-Magnetic Compatibility (EMC), antenna design and safety issues are covered in some depth.

When studying for the Advanced Radio Communications Examination there is currently no requirement to take a formal training course, this is because the examination is theory based and there is no practical training element in the syllabus. It is possible to study individually at home, but a number of technical colleges as well as local amateur radio clubs and societies runs courses specifically for the Advanced Radio Communications Examination. Alternatively, there are some correspondence and Internet courses available.

The Full licence allows access to all the UK amateur allocations with a maximum power limit of 400 watts on most bands. Like the Intermediate licence there are lower limits to the power that can be used on some bands: in the 135.7 - 137.8kHz band the power is limited to 1 watt ERP; between 1.850 and 2.000MHz it is 32 watts; 70.00 to 70.50MHz the power limit is 160 watts, and from 431 to 432MHz it is 40 watts ERP.

Callsigns in the M0 series are issued. These are changed to MI0, MM0, and MW0 etc dependent upon the country in which the station is located.

The UK Full amateur radio licence (© Ofcom. Image reproduced with permission).

The Full licence also has the advantage that it is recognised by many other countries and it can enable a reciprocal licence to be obtained with no requirement for taking an examination overseas.

## USING THE LICENCE

With the relevant pass certificate it is possible apply for a licence. This can be done through the Ofcom website (at http://www.ofcom.org.uk/licensing/olc/). It will require registering, and then entering the candidate number. As information is provided to Ofcom regarding the passes of examinations, it enables licences to be issued very swiftly. The precise callsign can be selected and the licence document can be downloaded.

With the licence and new callsign in hand, it is possible to go on the air. The first contact is always very memorable, although most people are a little nervous. However, it does not take long to get used to transmitting rather than listening and it is the next stage in appreciating the fascinating hobby of amateur radio. For many people it is a lifelong hobby that they find particularly stimulating and one in which they can make many friends.

Once established there are many different activities that can be tried. Many people enjoy a particular area of amateur radio but it is always worth trying some new avenue. In this way a lively interest can be maintained and a wide variety of activities explored. I have certainly enjoyed the hobby in a variety of areas and benefited greatly from it. I hope you do as well - good luck!

---

**FURTHER READING**

*Foundation Licence Now!* Alan Betts, G0HIQ, RSGB Revised 5th edn 2007.
*Intermediate Licence Book - Building on the Foundation*, Steve Hartley, G0FUW (ed), RSGB.
*Advance - The Full Licence Book*, Alan Betts, G0HIQ, and Steve Hartley, G0FUW, RSGB.
See also the Appendix for further contact addresses.

# Appendix

## SOURCES OF INFORMATION

General enquiries about amateur radio, amateur radio licence courses etc:
Radio Society of Great Britain
Lambda House
Cranborne Road
Potters Bar
EN6 3JE.
Tel: 0870 904 7373
Website: www.rsgb.org


UK amateur radio licence applications and information:
Website: www.ofcom.org.uk/licensing/olc/


Information about radio and electronics:
*Electronics and Radio Today* website: www.electronics-radio.com


Information about DX bands and operation, expeditions etc:
Website: www.dxbands.com


Amateur radio information:
Website: www.qrz.com


Amateur radio in the USA and the USA national society:
American Radio Relay League
225 Main Street
Newington
CT 06111-1494
USA.
Website: www.arrl.org

# Index

cooking class
# cakedecorating

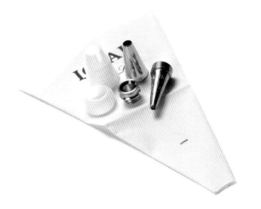

THE AUSTRALIAN
**Women's Weekly**

Making and decorating cakes for a special occasion — a child's birthday, a wedding, an anniversary, a baby shower — will give as much pleasure to you as it will to the lucky recipient. This splendid collection of cakes look difficult and impressive, but all of them can be made and decorated by a novice cakemaker (and anything you don't know can be found in the basic know-how chapter).

*Pamela Clark*

Food Director

NZ, Canada, US and UK readers Please note that Australian cup and spoon measurements are metric. A conversion chart appears on page 119.

34 cakes with easy step-by-step instructions

# contents

# wedded bliss

Suitable cakes: chocolate mud cake, page 102; white chocolate mud cake, page 104;
carrot cake, page 106; butter cake, page 108.

25cm round cake
22cm round cake
15cm round cake
3 quantities white
   chocolate ganache
4 cups (600g) white chocolate
   Melts, melted
1 bunch white hyacinths
florist tape

* ganache  page 116
* florist tape  page 114

1  Select and make the cakes.

2  Level the tops of all cakes so the cakes are the same height.

3  Centre 25cm cake, upside down, on plate.

4  Spread cake all over with about half of the ganache. Centre 22cm cake, upside down, on top of 25cm cake; spread cake all over with about two-thirds of the remaining ganache. Centre 15cm cake, upside down, on 22cm cake; spread cake all over with remaining ganache.

5  Spread about one-fifth of the chocolate onto a cold surface (such as marble); when set, drag a sharp knife over the surface of the chocolate to make curls. Repeat process using remaining chocolate.

6  Cover sides and top of cake with chocolate curls.

7  Bind ends of flowers with florist tape. Arrange flowers between tiers of cake.

tips  Lily of the valley, snow drops or star jasmine may be used as a substitute for hyacinths. We used a 30cm glass stand for this cake, but a prepared 30cm round board can be used instead. This cake can be completed (without flowers) 1 week ahead; keep refrigerated. Position flowers as late as possible. To serve this cake, remove the top tier first by carefully sliding large palette knives or egg slides under it. The curls will be slightly damaged. Separate the other tiers the same way.

spread chocolate onto cold surface

drag knife over chocolate to make curls

cover side of cake with chocolate curls

bind ends of hyacinths with florist ta

lemon delight

embrace optimism with this sunny cake, and will your wedding day to dawn fine

# lemon delight

Suitable cakes: fruit cake, page 100; chocolate mud cake, page 102;
white chocolate mud cake, page 104; carrot cake, page 106.

28cm round cake
20cm round cake
1/2 cup (80g) pure icing sugar,
   approximately
6kg prepared fondant
2cm high x 15cm round
   cardboard disk
1 egg white, beaten lightly
40cm round board
28cm round board
1 quantity sugar syrup
covered 20-gauge wire
20cm round board
2.5m x 7mm yellow satin ribbon
lemon-yellow colouring
1/2 quantity modelling fondant
cornflour
3cm fuchsia flower cutter
1 bundle ivory cake stamens
1 quantity royal icing
13g silver cachous

- prepared fondant  page 113
- board  page 112
- sugar syrup  page 110
- patching  page 111
- covering cake  page 113
- securing ribbon  page 114
- colouring  page 115
- modelling fondant  page 115
- ball tool  page 115
- templates  page 94
- royal icing  page 116
- piping bag  page 115

1   Select and make the cakes.

2   Level the tops of both cakes so the cakes are the same height.

3   On surface dusted with sifted icing sugar, knead 1.5kg of the prepared fondant until smooth; reserve one-third of the fondant, wrap both portions of fondant tightly in plastic wrap.

4   Brush disk with egg white. On surface dusted with sifted icing sugar, roll out reserved one-third of the fondant to 19cm round. Lift fondant over disk; with hands dusted with icing sugar, mould fondant around top and side of disk, trim edges. Leave overnight to set.

5   Brush 40cm board with egg white. On surface dusted with sifted icing sugar, roll out reserved 1kg of fondant to 40cm round. Lift fondant over board; trim edges. Leave overnight to set.

6   On surface dusted with sifted icing sugar, knead remaining 4.5kg fondant until smooth. Place 28cm cake, upside down, on 28cm board. Brush cake all over with sugar syrup. Patch and cover cake with two-thirds of the fondant. Place pin mark every 5cm along top and bottom edges of cake. To quilt, gently push wire into fondant, using pin marks as a guide, around side of cake. Repeat process with remaining fondant, 20cm cake and 20cm board.

7   Centre 28cm cake on fondant-covered board; centre fondant-covered disk on cake. Centre 20cm cake on disk. Secure ribbon around board and cakes.

8   On surface dusted with sifted icing sugar, knead colouring into modelling fondant, wrap tightly in plastic wrap. On surface dusted with cornflour, roll a little of the fondant to approximately 1mm thick, cover with plastic wrap. Cut flower out using 3cm fuchsia flower cutter, place flower in palm of hand dusted in cornflour, using ball tool, gently round petals and centre of flower. Place on tray lined with baking paper, leave to dry. Repeat process until you have 60 flowers. Repeat process using flower templates; you'll need five medium flowers and one large flower.

9   Cut stamens to 1cm in length. Place two-thirds of the royal icing into piping bag fitted with small star tube. Pipe small star of icing into flower, using tweezers, push about 3 stamens into icing. Repeat with remaining flowers and stamens. Leave about 30 minutes or until icing is set.

10   Place remaining icing into piping bag fitted with medium plain tube. Pipe several small dots of icing onto diamond pattern on cake, attach cachous with tweezers, repeat with more icing and cachous. Use remaining icing to secure flowers to cake.

tips   We used a cardboard lid to a round box for the disk, these are available from craft shops. Cake can be completed 1 week ahead.

cover disk with fondant

press wire gently into fondant

cut flowers out of modelling fondant

use ball tool to shape flower

use tweezers to attach stamens to flower

# hearts and flowers

Suitable cakes: fruit cake, page 100; chocolate mud cake, page 102;
white chocolate mud cake, page 104; carrot cake, page 106; butter cake, page 108.

30cm heart cake
¹/₂ cup (80g) pure icing sugar,
    approximately
2kg prepared fondant
lemon-yellow colouring
40cm heart-shaped board
1 quantity sugar syrup
1 bunch English lavender
1 bunch Italian lavender
1 bunch borage
florist tape
2m x 5cm each mauve and violet
    organza ribbons

- prepared fondant  page 113
- colouring  page 115
- board  page 112
- sugar syrup  page 110
- patching  page 111
- covering cake  page 113
- florist tape  page 114

1  Select and make the cake.

2  Level the top of the cake if necessary.

3  On surface dusted with sifted icing sugar, knead prepared fondant until smooth. Knead colouring into fondant, reserve one-quarter of the fondant; wrap tightly in plastic wrap. Wrap remaining fondant tightly in plastic wrap.

4  Centre cake, upside down, on board. Brush cake all over with sugar syrup. Patch and cover cake with remaining fondant.

5  Roll reserved fondant into 90cm sausage, shape around top edge of cake.

6  Bind ends of flowers with florist tape. Using a toothpick or skewer, push holes into sausage; insert flowers into holes to create wreath.

7  Secure ribbons around cake.

tips  Forget-me-nots can be used as an alternative to borage. Remove flowers before cutting the cake. Cake can be covered with fondant 1 week ahead; complete on day required.

shape fondant sausage around cake edge

bind ends of flowers with florist tape

insert flowers into holes in sausage

the decorated cake

# white on white

Suitable cakes: fruit cake, page 100; chocolate mud cake, page 102;
white chocolate mud cake, page 104; carrot cake, page 106; butter cake, page 108.

3 x 22cm round cakes
1¹/₂ cups (540g) apricot jam,
    warmed, strained, approximately
¹/₂ cup (80g) pure icing sugar,
    approximately
1kg prepared fondant
1 bunch silk gardenias

WHITE FROSTING
3 egg whites
4³/₄ cups (760g) icing
    sugar mixture
³/₄ teaspoon vegetable oil

• prepared fondant  page 113

1  Select and make the cakes.

2  Level the tops of all cakes so the cakes are the same height.

3  Sandwich cakes with some of the jam; brush side of cake with jam.

4  On surface dusted with sifted icing sugar, knead prepared fondant until smooth. Reserve one-quarter of the fondant; wrap fondant tightly in plastic wrap.

5  Measure height and circumference of cakes. Using this measurement, roll remaining fondant on surface dusted with sifted icing sugar into a strip; trim sides neatly.

6  Place side of cake on narrow end of fondant, roll cake along fondant to cover side of cake. Join ends of fondant with a little jam.

7  Centre cake on plate; trim top edge of fondant neatly with knife.

8  Brush top of cake with jam. Roll reserved fondant, on surface dusted with sifted icing sugar, into a circle just large enough to cover top of cake. Lift fondant onto cake; using fingers, mould edges together.

9  Using a small palette knife, spread side of cake with White Frosting.

10 Disassemble gardenias and leaves, you will need about 15 flowers for this cake. Arrange gardenias on cake.

White Frosting  Beat egg whites in small bowl with electric mixer until soft peaks form; gradually add icing sugar, beat until combined between additions. Add oil; beat until smooth.

tips  Cake can be completed 2 days ahead. If you prefer real flowers, tape the ends (page 114) and arrange them on cake an hour before required. We used a 30cm glass stand, but a prepared 30cm round board can be used instead.

roll cake along fondant strip

trim top edge of fondant

mould edges of fondant together

the decorated cake

# petals aplenty

Suitable cakes: carrot cake, page 106; butter cake, page 108.

25cm round cake
20cm round cake
2 quantities vienna cream
10 yellow roses
1 egg white, beaten lightly
1¹/₂ cups (330g) caster sugar
¹/₂ cup (110g) caster sugar, extra
yellow and orange colourings
¹/₄ cup (20g) baby white
    marshmallows, halved

* vienna cream  page 116
* coloured sugar  page 114
* colourings  page 115

1  Select and make the cakes.

2  Level the tops of both cakes so the cakes are the same height.

3  Centre 25cm cake, upside down, on plate.

4  Spread cake all over with about two-thirds of the vienna cream. Centre 20cm cake, upside down, on 25cm cake; spread cake all over with remaining cream.

5  Gently disassemble roses; brush each petal and leaf sparingly with egg white, sprinkle both sides of petals and leaves sparingly with sugar, tap off any excess sugar.

6  Place petals and leaves on wire rack to dry for about 30 minutes.

7  Position petals on cake to recreate flower shapes, decorate with leaves.

8  To colour sugar, place extra sugar in small plastic bag with colourings, rub together to combine.

9  Brush marshmallows lightly with egg white; dip marshmallows into coloured sugar, position in centres of flowers.

tips  We used a 30cm glass stand for this cake, but a prepared 30cm round board can be used instead. Use roses of any colour; simply tint the sugar the same colour as the petals. Remove the top tier by sliding large palette knives or egg slides between the cakes. Remove petals before cutting cake. Ice and decorate cake on day required.

disassemble roses

brush petals with egg white

sprinkle petals on both sides with sugar

the decorated cake

*gift-wrapped*

*a time for giving... show how much you care with this tiered triumph*

# gift-wrapped

Suitable cakes: fruit cake, page 100; chocolate mud cake, page 102; white chocolate mud cake, page 104.

30cm square cake
19cm square cake
15cm square cake
1/2 cup (80g) pure icing
    sugar, approximately
6kg prepared fondant
30cm square board
1 quantity sugar syrup
19cm square board
15cm square board
35cm square board
6 butcher's wooden
    skewers
2.8m white ric rac braid
aqua colouring
2cm, 1.5cm, 1cm, 5mm
    round cutters

- prepared fondant  page 113
- board  page 112
- sugar syrup  page 110
- patching  page 111
- covering cake  page 113
- butcher's wooden
  skewers  page 99
- securing braid  page 114
- colourings  page 115

1  Select and make the cakes.

2  Level the tops of all cakes so the cakes are the same height.

3  On surface dusted with sifted icing sugar, knead prepared fondant until smooth. Reserve 1kg of the fondant, wrap tightly in plastic wrap. Wrap remaining fondant tightly in plastic wrap.

4  Place 30cm cake, upside down, on 30cm board. Brush cake all over with sugar syrup. Patch and cover cake with half of the fondant. Repeat process with two-thirds of the remaining fondant, 19cm cake and 19cm board, then remaining fondant, 15cm cake and 15cm board. Reserve fondant scraps; wrap tightly in plastic wrap.

5  Place pin mark every 4cm along top and bottom of 30cm cake; dust pastry wheel with sifted icing sugar. Using pin marks as a guide, gently push edge of wheel into side of fondant, roll wheel to form a zig-zag pattern.

6  Centre 30cm cake on 35cm board. Insert 3 butcher's wooden skewers towards centre of 30cm cake, positioned to support the 19cm cake; trim skewers to make them level with top surface of cake. Repeat process with 19cm cake and remaining skewers. Centre 19cm cake on 30cm cake; centre 15cm cake on top.

7  Secure ric rac braid around cakes.

8  On surface dusted with sifted icing sugar, knead colouring into reserved fondant. Reserve two-thirds of aqua fondant, wrap tightly in plastic wrap.

9  For the dots: On surface dusted with sifted icing sugar, roll one-third of aqua fondant to about 5mm thick; cut out 20 rounds using 2cm cutter, 20 rounds using 1.5cm cutter, 20 rounds using 1cm cutter and 70 rounds using 5mm cutter. Roll reserved scraps of white fondant to about 5mm thick; cut out 25 rounds using 5mm cutter. Place rounds on tray lined with baking paper, leave about 30 minutes or until dry.

10 Brush aqua 5mm dots with sugar syrup on one side, attach to bottom tier of cake over pin marks. Repeat process with remaining aqua and white dots to middle tier of cake.

11 For the bow: On surface dusted with sifted icing sugar, roll reserved aqua fondant until it forms rectangle approximately 18.5cm x 45cm and about 5mm thick; cut into five 3.5cm strips, cut v-shapes into both ends of strips, lightly brush sugar syrup on one side of two strips, drape wet side of strips over top tier of cake. With two of the remaining strips of fondant, form cross, fold into bow shape, using cotton wool balls to keep in position. With remaining strip of fondant, make two loops, use cotton wool balls to keep in position; attach loops with sugar syrup in centre of bow. Place bow on tray lined with baking paper, stand overnight to dry. Remove cotton wool from bow; place bow on cake.

tip  Cake can be completed 1 week ahead.

use pastry wheel for zig-zag pattern

attach dots to side of cake

drape fondant strips over top tier

shape bow from fondant strips

# coming up daisies

Suitable cakes: fruit cake, page 100; chocolate mud cake, page 102;
white chocolate mud cake, page 104; carrot cake, page 106; butter cake, page 108.

25cm round cake
17cm round cake
$^1/_2$ cup (80g) pure icing sugar,
    approximately
2.5kg prepared fondant
25cm round board
1 quantity sugar syrup
17cm round board
3 butcher's wooden skewers
20cm plastic cake stand
2 bunches daisies
florist tape
1.2m x 1.5cm yellow check ribbon

- prepared fondant  page 113
- board  page 112
- sugar syrup  page 110
- patching  page 111
- covering cake  page 113
- butcher's wooden
  skewers  page 99
- florist tape  page 114
- securing ribbon  page 114

1 Select and make the cakes.

2 Level the tops of both cakes so the cakes are the same height.

3 On surface dusted with sifted icing sugar, knead prepared fondant until smooth. Reserve a piece of fondant the size of a golf ball, wrap tightly in plastic wrap; wrap remaining fondant tightly in plastic wrap.

4 Centre 25cm cake, upside down, on 25cm board. Brush cake all over with sugar syrup. Patch and cover cake with two-thirds of the remaining fondant. Repeat with remaining fondant, 17cm cake and 17cm board.

5 Insert butcher's wooden skewers towards centre of 25cm cake, positioned to support the 17cm cake; trim skewers to make them level with top surface of cake.

6 Place 25cm cake on plastic cake stand; centre on plate.

7 Centre 17cm cake on 25cm cake.

8 Roll reserved fondant into ball, place in centre of top of cake.

9 Bind ends of flowers with florist tape. Insert flowers into ball of fondant. Arrange remaining flowers around base of cake.

10 Secure ribbon around cake.

tips We used fresh daisies for this cake, but artificial flowers are also fine. The plastic cake stand is used to elevate the cake slightly; any suitable sized plastic plate can be used. We used a 30cm glass stand for this cake, but a prepared 30cm round board can be used instead. If using fresh flowers, arrange them on the cake just before required. The cake (without fresh flowers) can be completed 1 week ahead.

place 25cm cake onto plastic stand

place ball of fondant on top of cake

bind ends of flowers with florist tape

the decorated cake

# ribbons 'n' roses

timelessly elegant with a modern twist... it's all in the cornelli detailing and artful ribbon work

# ribbons 'n' roses

Suitable cakes: fruit cake, page 100; chocolate mud cake, page 102; white chocolate mud cake, page 104.

2 x 19cm square cakes
15cm square cake
1/2 cup (80g) pure icing
    sugar, approximately
4kg prepared fondant
ivory colouring
1/3 cup (120g) apricot jam, warmed,
    strained
26cm square board
1 quantity sugar syrup
15cm square board
3 butcher's wooden skewers
1/2 quantity modelling fondant
cornflour
2cm 5-petal blossom cutter
1 quantity royal icing
13g silver cachous
6.5m x 3.5cm ivory satin ribbon
5 roses

- prepared fondant  page 113
- colourings  page 115
- board  page 112
- sugar syrup  page 110
- patching  page 111
- covering cake  page 113
- butcher's wooden
  skewers  page 99
- modelling fondant  page 115
- royal icing  page 116
- piping bag  page 115
- securing ribbon  page 114

1 Select and make the cakes.

2 Level the tops of all cakes so the cakes are the same height.

3 On surface dusted with sifted icing sugar, knead prepared fondant until smooth. Knead colouring into fondant; wrap tightly in plastic wrap.

4 Sandwich 19cm cakes with jam. Centre cake, upside down, on 26cm board. Brush cake all over with sugar syrup. Patch and cover cake with two-thirds of the fondant. Repeat process with remaining fondant, 15cm cake and 15cm board.

5 Insert butcher's wooden skewers towards centre of 19cm cake, positioned to support 15cm cake; trim skewers to make level with top surface of cake. Centre 15cm cake on 19cm cake.

6 On surface dusted with sifted icing sugar, knead modelling fondant until smooth. Knead colouring into fondant. On surface dusted with cornflour, roll fondant to approximately 1.5mm thick. Using cutter, cut out a blossom shape; cover remaining fondant with plastic wrap to prevent drying. Using fingers, shape petals upward, leave to dry. Repeat process with remaining fondant. You will need 28 blossoms for this cake.

7 Lightly mark cake with pin in centre of each side of cake where ribbon will finish. Tint royal icing using colouring. Place icing into piping bag fitted with medium plain tube. Pipe continuous line in cornelli pattern over sides of cake extending down to pin mark.

8 With remaining icing, pipe small dot of icing into centre of a blossom. Using tweezers, place a cachou on icing. Repeat with remaining blossoms and cachous.

9 Pipe a small dot of icing on a corner of one cake, attach blossom to cake. Repeat with icing and remaining blossoms.

10 Cut five 80cm and five 12cm lengths of ribbon; secure remaining ribbon around 15cm cake and 19cm cake. Accordion-pleat 80cm ribbon to create bow, attach 12cm ribbon to end, secure with icing and pin; leave 15 minutes for icing to set, remove pin. Repeat with remaining ribbons. Attach bows to cake with icing.

11 Arrange roses on cake.

tips We used "Julia" roses for this cake; place on the cake just before required. The cake (without flowers) can be completed 1 week ahead.

shape petals of cut-out blossoms

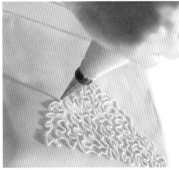

pipe cornelli pattern onto cake

attach blossoms to cake

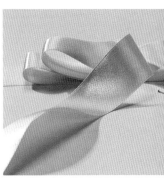

accordion-pleat ribbon

birthdays

# choc star

Suitable cakes: chocolate mud cake, page 102; white chocolate mud cake, page 104.

19cm square cake
30cm square cake
48cm star board
2 quantities chocolate ganache
2 cups (300g) dark chocolate
    Melts, melted
2 teaspoons vegetable oil
1¹/₂ cups (225g) white chocolate
    Melts, melted

• template  page 94
• board  page 112
• ganache  page 116

1  Select and make the cakes.

2  Level the tops of both cakes so the cakes are the same height.

3  Using template as a guide, cut out shapes from cakes.

4  Arrange cake pieces in star shape, upside down, on board.

5  Spread cake all over with ganache.

6  Combine dark chocolate and 1 teaspoon of the oil in small bowl.
   Spread about half of the chocolate onto a cold surface (such as marble);
   when set, drag an ice-cream scoop over the surface of the chocolate to
   make curls. Repeat process using remaining chocolate.

7  Combine white chocolate and remaining oil in small bowl. Repeat
   process as above.

8  Cover top of cake with chocolate curls.

   tips  A 40cm square board can be used instead of a star-shaped board. Curls
   can be made 1 week ahead; keep in airtight container in cool, dark place.
   Cake can be completed 1 week ahead; keep refrigerated.

cut cake using template as a guide

make chocolate curls

the decorated cake

# chocolate box

This magnificent cake is a gift beyond compare for somebody extra-special

# chocolate box

Suitable cakes: chocolate mud cake, page 102; white chocolate mud cake, page 104;
carrot cake, page 106; butter cake, page 108.

2 x 15cm square cakes
1 quantity chocolate ganache
1kg (8 cups) white chocolate
    Melts, melted
gold lustre colour
2.2m x 5cm purple organza ribbon
3m x 4cm gold heart
    organza ribbon
37cm square board
20cm x 5mm gold satin ribbon

- ganache  page 116
- piping bag  page 115
- template  page 94
- colourings  page 115
- board  page 112

1  Select and make the cakes.

2  Level the tops of both cakes so the cakes are the same height.

3  Sandwich cakes with a little of the ganache. Spread cake all over with remaining ganache.

4  Draw five 17cm squares, one 18.5cm square and four 5cm x 18cm rectangles onto baking paper; turn paper over so drawing is underneath.

5  Place one-eighth of the melted chocolate into piping bag; reserve. Spread remaining chocolate over all the squares and rectangles on the baking paper sheets. Stand chocolate about 10 minutes or until almost set.

6  Using a sharp knife, trim edges of chocolate.

7  Using template as a guide, trace eight scroll patterns and one heart onto baking paper, turn paper over so drawing is underneath. Pipe scrolls and heart onto baking paper using reserved chocolate; leave about 5 minutes or until almost set. Paint scrolls and heart with gold lustre colour. Gently remove the five squares from baking paper. Gently lift scrolls off paper, carefully position two scrolls each onto the smooth underside of four of the 17cm chocolate squares, secure scrolls with a little of the piped reserved chocolate.

8  To make lid, gently remove 18.5cm square from paper, invert. Using remaining chocolate, pipe along edge of square, attach rectangles to square. Support sides with straight-sided dish. Stand about 10 minutes or until set.

9  Divide purple and gold heart ribbons in half. Position ribbons, diagonally crossed, on board. Centre remaining 17cm chocolate square on ribbons. Centre cake on chocolate. Using remaining chocolate, pipe along edges of square, attach decorated sides, support with straight-sided dishes until chocolate is set.

10 Position chocolate lid on box. Bring ribbon up sides of cake, tie ribbon in bow on top of cake. Attach chocolate heart to cake with gold ribbon.

tips  Paint gold lustre colour onto chocolate scrolls and heart when the chocolate is almost set – the gold will be easier to apply. Gold lustre colour is inedible. If chocolate squares are difficult to cut, heat the blade of the sharp knife under very hot water; dry knife and use while hot. Cake can be completed 1 week ahead; keep refrigerated.

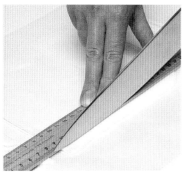

trim sides of chocolate with sharp knife

pipe chocolate scrolls onto baking paper

paint gold lustre colour onto chocolate

assemble chocolate box lid

# good sport

Suitable cakes: chocolate mud cake, page 102; white chocolate mud cake, page 104; carrot cake, page 106; butter cake, page 108.

26cm octagonal cake
1¹/₂ quantities white
    chocolate ganache
35cm round board
1 cup (150g) dark chocolate
    Melts, melted
3 cups (450g) white chocolate
    Melts, melted
orange, green and red colourings
3 teaspoons vegetable oil
24 red golf tees
24 soccer ball candles

- board  page 112
- ganache  page 116
- piping bag  page 115
- colourings  page 115

1  Select and make the cake.

2  Level the top of cake if necessary.

3  Centre cake, upside down, on board. Spread cake all over with ganache.

4  Cut baking paper into two strips measuring 8cm x 48cm. Divide each strip into 6cm segments, draw sporting designs in each segment onto baking paper; turn paper over so drawing is underneath.

5  Place dark chocolate in piping bag, pipe chocolate onto paper, using drawings as a guide.

6  Divide ¹/₂ cup of the white chocolate into three small bowls, reserve remaining chocolate. Using colouring, tint one-third of the chocolate orange, stir in 1 teaspoon of the oil. Place orange chocolate into piping bag, pipe balls onto baking paper. Repeat process with remaining two-thirds of chocolate with red and green colourings and oil.

7  Spread reserved chocolate evenly over the designs on the baking paper; leave about 5 minutes or until chocolate is almost set. Using sharp knife, cut chocolate into 6cm panels. Gently peel away baking paper.

8  Place chocolate panels around side of cake.

9  Arrange golf tees and candles on cake.

tips  If you prefer, this cake can feature a single sporting motif of your choice. Cake can be made 1 week ahead; keep refrigerated.

pipe chocolate designs onto paper

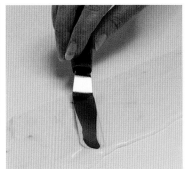
spread white chocolate over paper

cut chocolate into 6cm panels

the decorated cake

# bar mitzvah

Suitable cakes: fruit cake, page 100; chocolate mud cake, page 102;
white chocolate mud cake, page 104; carrot cake, page 106; butter cake, page 108.

23cm square cake
1/2 cup (80g) pure icing sugar,
   approximately
2kg prepared fondant
violet and royal-blue colouring
35cm square board
1 quantity sugar syrup
3.5cm star cutter

- prepared fondant  page 113
- colourings  page 115
- board  page 112
- sugar syrup  page 110
- patching  page 111
- covering cake  page 113

1 Select and make the cake.

2 Level the top of the cake if necessary.

3 On surface dusted with icing sugar, knead prepared fondant until smooth.
Reserve 500g of fondant; wrap tightly in plastic wrap. Knead violet and
royal-blue colouring into remaining fondant; wrap tightly in plastic wrap.

4 Centre cake, upside down, on board. Brush cake all over with sugar
syrup. Patch and cover cake with blue fondant.

5 Roll reserved fondant onto surface dusted with sifted icing sugar into
a strip measuring 8cm x 60cm; trim edges neatly. Mark fondant along
long sides of strip; mark 4.3cm along one long side, then continue
marking at 8.6cm intervals to the end. Mark other long side of fondant
at 8.6cm intervals. Using markings as a guide, cut fondant into triangles.
Using star cutter, cut stars out of centres of triangles; place stars on tray
lined with baking paper, leave to dry.

6 Lightly brush sugar syrup onto backs of triangles, attach to sides of cake.
Lightly brush backs of stars with sugar syrup, attach to top of cake.

tip Cake can be completed 1 week ahead.

cut fondant into triangles

cut star shapes from triangles

attach triangles to cake

the decorated cake

# meringue surprise

5 egg whites
1¹/₄ cups (275g) caster sugar
¹/₂ cup (55g) hazelnut meal
600ml thickened cream
¹/₃ cup (110g) Nutella
1¹/₂ tablespoons cocoa powder
1 cup (150g) dark chocolate
    Melts, melted
1 cup (150g) white chocolate
    Melts, melted
brown Smarties
brown baby M&M's

• piping bag  page 115

1  Beat egg whites in medium bowl with electric mixer until soft peaks form. Add sugar, in batches, beating until dissolved between additions. Gently fold hazelnut meal into meringue mixture.

2  Line three oven trays with baking paper, trace a 20cm circle onto each sheet of baking paper. Place meringue mixture into a piping bag fitted with 1.5cm plain tube. Starting from the centre, pipe meringue in concentric circles to cover each marked circle. Bake in slow oven about 1 hour or until meringue is crisp. Cool in oven with door ajar.

3  Reserve ³/₄ cup (180ml) of the cream. Beat remaining cream, Nutella and sifted cocoa in small bowl with electric mixer until firm peaks form.

4  Gently lift meringues off paper, centre a layer on serving plate. Spread half of the cream mixture over meringue, continue layering with remaining meringue and cream mixture, finishing with meringue.

5  Beat reserved cream in small bowl with electric mixer until soft peaks form. Spread over top of cake.

6  Place dark chocolate and white chocolate in separate piping bags, snip a tiny hole in each bag. On tray lined with baking paper, use both chocolates to pipe flower shapes in varying sizes. Fill in centres of flowers using both chocolates. Attach Smarties and M&M's to half the flowers before chocolate is set. Leave about 5 minutes or until chocolate is set. Carefully lift flowers off paper. Arrange on top and side of cake.

tips  We used a 30cm glass stand for this cake, but a prepared 30cm round board can be used instead. This cake is perfect as a dessert or to have with coffee, and is best made the day before serving.

pipe meringue in concentric circle

pipe flower shapes with chocolate

pipe chocolate inside flowers

the decorated cake

# free-form fantasy

Suitable cakes: chocolate mud cake, page 102; white chocolate mud cake, page 104.

22cm round cake
1 quantity chocolate ganache
2 cups (300g) dark chocolate Melts
1/3 cup (80ml) light corn syrup
2 tablespoons icing sugar mixture
30 assorted chocolates
2 teaspoons cocoa powder

• ganache page 116

1 Select and make the cake.

2 Level the top of the cake if necessary.

3 Centre cake, upside down, on plate.

4 Spread cake all over with ganache.

5 Melt chocolate in medium bowl placed over hot water; add corn syrup, stir until mixture becomes thick and slightly grainy. Cover with plastic wrap, stand about 3 hours or until mixture becomes firm.

6 On surface dusted with sifted icing sugar, knead modelling chocolate until smooth. Roll chocolate between sheets of baking paper until large enough to cover cake all over, plus another 10cm to allow for folds.

7 Drape chocolate over cake, gently lifting and easing chocolate into folds, trim edge.

8 Arrange chocolates on cake. Dust cake with sifted cocoa.

tips We used a 30cm glass stand for this cake, but a prepared 30cm round board can be used instead. Modelling chocolate is also suitable for moulding flowers and leaves. Cake can be completed 1 week ahead; keep refrigerated.

add corn syrup to melted chocolate

knead modelling chocolate until smooth

ease chocolate into decorative folds

the decorated cake

# tiramisu with a twist

8 eggs
1¹/₃ cups (300g) caster sugar
²/₃ cup (100g) cornflour
²/₃ cup (100g) plain flour
²/₃ cup (100g) self-raising flour
³/₄ cup (180ml) boiling water
2 tablespoons instant
   coffee powder
³/₄ cup (180ml) marsala
300ml thickened cream
¹/₃ cup (55g) icing sugar mixture
2 cups (500g) mascarpone
40cm x 45cm board
600ml thickened cream, extra
750g strawberries, halved
2 cups (160g) flaked
   almonds, toasted
1 cup (220g) caster sugar, extra
¹/₄ cup (60ml) cold water

• board page 112

1 Grease 28cm x 34cm baking dish, line base with baking paper.

2 Beat eggs and sugar in large bowl with electric mixer about 10 minutes or until very thick and pale. Gently fold triple-sifted flours into egg mixture. Pour into prepared pan. Bake in moderate oven 40 minutes. Turn cake onto wire rack to cool.

3 Meanwhile, combine boiling water and coffee in small bowl; stir to dissolve, add marsala.

4 Beat cream and icing sugar in small bowl with electric mixer until soft peaks form; stir in mascarpone and ¹/₂ cup of the coffee mixture.

5 Split cold cake into three layers. Centre one layer of cake on board, brush top with one-third of the remaining coffee mixture, spread with half of the cream mixture. Repeat layering with second layer of cake, half of the remaining coffee mixture and remaining cream mixture. Finish with cake layer and remaining coffee mixture.

6 Beat extra cream in small bowl with electric mixer until soft peaks form. Spread cake all over with cream. Refrigerate overnight.

7 Position strawberries on top and sides of cake. Sprinkle almonds on cake in diamond pattern.

8 Place extra sugar and cold water in small saucepan; stir over heat until sugar dissolves. Boil, uncovered, without stirring, about 10 minutes or until syrup is golden. Remove from heat, allow bubbles to subside. Using teaspoon, drizzle hot toffee carefully over almonds.

tips This cake is ideal as a dessert for a party, as it will serve at least 12 people. Assemble the cake, covered with cream, and refrigerate the day before required. Decorate cake with strawberries, almonds and toffee about 2 hours before serving.

brush coffee mixture over cake

drizzle toffee over almonds

the decorated cake

# pumpkin patch

Suitable cakes: fruit cake, page 100; chocolate mud cake, page 102;
white chocolate mud cake, page 104; carrot cake, page 106; butter cake, page 108.

25cm round cake
1/2 cup (80g) pure icing sugar,
  approximately
1.5kg prepared fondant
35cm round board
1 quantity sugar syrup
green colouring
500g prepared almond icing
orange colouring
paper florist tape
ivy leaves
1 teaspoon vegetable oil
1/2 cup (75g) dark chocolate
  Melts, melted
3m natural-coloured raffia

* prepared fondant  page 113
* board  page 112
* sugar syrup  page 110
* patching  page 111
* covering cake  page 113
* colourings  page 115
* prepared almond icing  page 110

1 Select and make the cake.

2 Level the top of the cake if necessary.

3 On surface dusted with sifted icing sugar, knead prepared fondant until smooth; wrap fondant tightly in plastic wrap.

4 Centre cake, upside down, on board. Brush cake all over with sugar syrup. Patch and cover cake with fondant.

5 On surface dusted with sifted icing sugar, knead green colouring into golf-ball-sized piece of prepared almond icing; wrap tightly in plastic wrap. Tint remaining almond icing with orange colouring, wrap tightly in plastic wrap. Roll varying-sized pieces of orange almond icing into balls; gently flatten top and bottom. With toothpick or skewer, gently press vertical lines into almond icing balls to make pumpkin shapes. Using green almond icing, mould tiny stalk shapes for each pumpkin. Brush tops of pumpkins with water, position stalks.

6 Cut tape in half lengthways, stretch and twist tape. Wind tape around toothpicks or skewers to make tendrils. Using a skewer or toothpick push tendrils gently into pumpkins close to stalks. Place pumpkins on tray lined with baking paper, leave to dry.

7 Wash and dry ivy leaves carefully. Lightly brush the tops of the leaves with oil. Brush chocolate evenly onto oiled side of leaves, leave about 10 minutes or until chocolate is set. Carefully peel leaves from chocolate.

8 Twist raffia into long rope, tie raffia around cake. Decorate cake with pumpkins, chocolate ivy leaves and fresh ivy leaves.

tips You could buy marzipan fruit or use daisies to decorate this cake. Cake can be completed 1 week ahead. This cake makes a delightful Halloween treat.

use toothpick to mark pumpkins

stretch and twist paper florist tape

wind twisted tape around toothpick

brush melted chocolate onto ivy leaves

# double up

perfectly splendid... your breath will catch when you see this cheerful pile of presents

# double up

Suitable cakes: fruit cake, page 100; chocolate mud cake, page 102;
white chocolate mud cake, page 104; carrot cake, page 106; butter cake, page 108.

28cm square cake
19cm square cake
1/2 cup (80g) pure icing sugar,
    approximately
4kg prepared fondant
rose-pink and orange colourings
28cm square board
1 quantity sugar syrup
19cm square board
3 butcher's wooden skewers
2m x 5cm each hot pink and orange
    organza ribbon
40cm square board
1 quantity modelling fondant
aqua-blue, green and
    purple colourings
cornflour
4cm heart, 5-petal flower, 4cm star
    and daisy cutters
covered 22-gauge wire
7mm flower cutter
1cm blossom cutter
1/2 quantity royal icing
375g packet baby M&M's
1m x 5cm each purple and lime
    organza ribbon
1m x 2cm each pink and orange
    organza ribbon

- prepared fondant  page 113
- colourings  page 115
- board  page 112
- sugar syrup  page 110
- patching  page 111
- covering cake  page 113
- butcher's wooden
  skewers  page 99
- modelling fondant  page 115
- royal icing  page 116
- piping bag  page 115

1  Select and make the cakes.

2  Level the tops of both cakes so the cakes are the same height.

3  On surface dusted with sifted icing sugar, knead two-thirds of the
prepared fondant until smooth. Knead pink colouring into fondant;
wrap tightly in plastic wrap. Knead orange colouring into remaining
one-third of fondant; wrap tightly in plastic wrap.

4  Place 28cm cake, upside down, on 28cm board. Brush cake all over
with sugar syrup. Patch and cover cake with pink fondant. Repeat
process with 19cm cake, 19cm board and orange fondant.

5  Insert three butcher's wooden skewers towards centre of 28cm cake,
positioned to support the 19cm cake; trim skewers to make them level
with top surface of cake.

6  Cut two 50cm lengths from the 5cm-wide pink ribbon, position ribbons
on 28cm cake, tucking ends under cake. Centre cake on 40cm board. Cut
two 40cm lengths from the 5cm-wide orange ribbon, repeat process on
19cm cake. Position 19cm cake on 28cm cake.

7  On surface dusted with sifted icing sugar, knead modelling fondant until
smooth. Knead aqua-blue colouring into one-quarter of the fondant,
green colouring into one-quarter of the fondant and purple colouring into
one-quarter of the fondant; wrap tightly in plastic wrap. Divide remaining
fondant in half, knead pink colouring into one-half of the fondant and
orange colouring into other half; wrap tightly in plastic wrap.

8  On surface dusted with cornflour, and using one portion of fondant at
a time, roll out to 5mm thickness. Using the heart, flower, star and daisy
cutters, cut out shapes using the different coloured fondants – use our
finished cake as a guide. Insert a length of damp wire into each shape as
you cut it out, leave on tray lined with baking paper to dry.

9  Using the flower and blossom cutters, cut out shapes using the
remaining coloured fondant and any scraps left over from the larger
shapes. Leave on tray lined with baking paper to dry.

10 Tint royal icing pink, place into piping bag fitted with medium plain tube.
Combine about half of the dried small fondant shapes with M&M's,
gently scatter over tops of cakes. Pipe small dots of icing onto backs
of remaining fondant shapes and M&M's, attach to sides of cakes.

11 Make large bow with remaining pieces of ribbon, secure with wire,
place on top of cake. Cut wires of dried large fondant shapes to desired
lengths, arrange on cake.

tip  Tape the ends of the wired shapes if inserting into the cake. Mix and
match colours of fondants, decorations and ribbons to suit your own taste.
Cake can be completed 1 week ahead.

tuck ends of ribbons under cake

insert damp wire into large shapes

cut out small shapes

make bow from ribbon

special occasions

# berry christmas

Suitable cakes: fruit cake, page 100; chocolate mud cake, page 102;
white chocolate mud cake, page 104; carrot cake, page 106; butter cake, page 108.

25cm round cake
1/4 cup (40g) pure icing sugar,
   approximately
500g prepared fondant
1 quantity sugar syrup
1 quantity fluffy frosting
packaging tape
1.25m x 5cm green velvet ribbon
250g fresh red currants
1 bunch holly leaves

- prepared fondant  page 113
- sugar syrup  page 110
- fluffy frosting  page 117
- securing ribbon  page 114

1  Select and make the cake.

2  Level the top of the cake if necessary.

3  Cut 12cm circle of baking paper. Centre paper on cake; cut out centre of cake using paper as a guide.

4  On surface dusted with sifted icing sugar, knead prepared fondant until smooth; wrap tightly in plastic wrap.

5  Centre cake, upside down, on plate. Brush top with sugar syrup. Roll fondant to about a 20cm round. Lift fondant onto cake, use fingers to gently ease fondant to edges of cake; trim edges, cut out centre.

6  Spread fluffy frosting over fondant.

7  Stick packaging tape to back of ribbon to prevent cake from staining ribbon. Secure ribbon around cake, secure remaining ribbon on cut inside of cake.

8  Arrange red currants and holly leaves on cake.

   tips  We used a 30cm glass stand for this cake, but a prepared 30cm round board can be used instead. If red currants are unavailable, any berries can be substituted. Artificial holly can be used in place of the fresh holly leaves. Cake is best completed on day of serving.

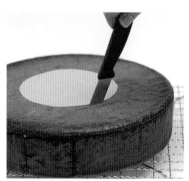
cut circle from centre of cake

spread frosting over fondant

sticking tape to back of ribbon

the decorated cake

# sweet dreams

Suitable cakes: chocolate mud cake, page 102; white chocolate mud cake, page 104; carrot cake, page 106; butter cake, page 108.

30cm heart cake
40cm heart-shaped board
2 quantities vienna cream
3 cups (450g) white chocolate
   Melts, melted
rose-pink colouring
1 bunch pink roses

• board  page 112
• vienna cream  page 116
• colourings  page 115
• piping bag  page 115

1  Select and make the cake.

2  Level the top of the cake if necessary.

3  Centre cake, upside down, on board.

4  Spread cake all over with vienna cream.

5  Reserve one-third of the chocolate in small bowl. Using colouring, tint remaining chocolate pink; reserve half of the pink chocolate in small bowl. Spread remaining chocolate onto cold surface (such as marble); drag a pastry comb through unset chocolate, leave about 5 minutes or until almost set. Spread reserved white chocolate over pink chocolate. When chocolate is set, drag a sharp knife over the surface of the chocolate to make curls.

6  Place reserved pink chocolate in piping bag. On tray lined with baking paper, pipe heart shapes; leave to set. Gently lift hearts off paper; position around side of cake.

7  Remove petals from roses. Arrange petals and chocolate curls on cake.

tips  Use insecticide-free roses. Chocolate curls can be made 1 week ahead. Ice and decorate cake several hours before required.

drag pastry comb through pink chocolate

spread white chocolate onto pink

drag knife over chocolate to make curls

position hearts on side of cake

the decorated cake

# native beauty

Suitable cakes: fruit cake, page 100; chocolate mud cake, page 102;
white chocolate mud cake, page 104; carrot cake, page 106; butter cake, page 108.

26cm octagonal cake
17cm octagonal cake
1/2 cup (80g) pure icing sugar,
    approximately
2.5kg prepared fondant
daffodil-yellow colouring
35cm octagonal board
1 quantity sugar syrup
17cm octagonal board
3 butcher's wooden skewers
silk flannel flowers
covered 24-gauge wire
florist tape

* prepared fondant  page 113
* colourings  page 115
* board  page 112
* sugar syrup  page 110
* patching  page 111
* covering cake  page 113
* butcher's wooden
    skewers  page 99
* florist tape  page 114

1  Select and make the cakes.

2  Level the tops of both cakes so the cakes are the same height.

3  On surface dusted with sifted icing sugar, knead prepared fondant until
   smooth. Knead colouring into fondant; wrap tightly in plastic wrap.

4  Centre 26cm cake, upside down, on 35cm board. Brush cake all over with
   sugar syrup. Patch and cover cake with two-thirds of the fondant. Repeat
   process with remaining fondant, 17cm cake and 17cm board.

5  Insert butcher's wooden skewers towards centre of 26cm cake,
   positioned to support the 17cm cake; trim skewers to make them level
   with top surface of cake. Centre 17cm cake on 26cm cake.

6  Disassemble flannel flowers and leaves; wire and tape ends of flowers
   and leaves together. Arrange flowers and leaves on cake.

   tip  Cake can be completed 1 week ahead.

wire and tape flowers and leaves

the decorated cake

# it's a boy

Suitable cakes: fruit cake, page 100; chocolate mud cake, page 102;
white chocolate mud cake, page 104; carrot cake, page 106; butter cake, page 108.

23cm square cake
1/2 cup (80g) pure icing sugar,
   approximately
3.5kg prepared fondant
cornflower-blue colouring
35cm square board
1 quantity sugar syrup
brown colouring
teddy bear chocolate mould
cornflour
1/2 quantity royal icing

- prepared fondant  page 113
- colourings  page 115
- board  page 112
- sugar syrup  page 110
- patching  page 111
- covering cake  page 113
- ball tool  page 115
- royal icing  page 116
- piping bag  page 115

1  Select and make the cake.

2  Level the top of the cake if necessary.

3  On surface dusted with sifted icing sugar, knead prepared fondant until smooth. Reserve 500g of fondant; wrap tightly in plastic wrap. Knead blue colouring into remaining fondant; divide fondant in half, wrap tightly in plastic wrap.

4  Centre cake, upside down, on board. Brush cake all over with sugar syrup. Patch and cover cake with half of the blue fondant.

5  On surface dusted with sifted icing sugar, roll remaining blue fondant to about 40cm square; trim edges to make square. Using a ruler, mark 3cm intervals around all four edges. Using pastry wheel, ruler and markings as a guide, gently push edge of wheel into fondant, roll wheel to quilt.

6  Using a ball tool, ruffle the edges of fondant to resemble a frill.

7  Brush cake all over with sugar syrup. Carefully drape fondant over cake.

8  On surface dusted with sifted icing sugar, roll three-quarters of reserved fondant to about 10cm square; trim edges to make square. Using a ball tool, ruffle edges of fondant to resemble a frill. Place pillow on tray lined with baking paper, allow to dry.

9  On surface dusted with sifted icing sugar, knead brown colouring into remaining fondant. Dust teddy bear mould with cornflour; push fondant into mould, carefully remove fondant, trim edges. Place bear on tray lined with baking paper, allow to dry.

10 Tint royal icing blue, place icing in small piping bag. Secure bear to pillow with a little icing. Attach pillow to cake with icing; pipe child's name on pillow .

11 Pipe star and heart shapes onto cake with remaining icing.

   tip  This cake is suitable for a boy or a girl. For an extra touch, real lace can be tucked under the pillow. Cake can be completed 1 week ahead.

quilt fondant with pastry wheel

drape quilted fondant over cake

ruffle edges of pillow with ball tool

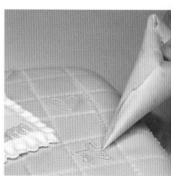
pipe star and heart shapes

# hazelnut berry beauty

500g butter, chopped
4 cups (880g) caster sugar
12 eggs
2 cups (300g) plain flour
1 cup (150g) self-raising flour
2 cups (220g) hazelnut meal
300g sour cream
300g fresh or frozen raspberries
300g fresh or frozen blackberries
2 quantities white
    chocolate ganache
3 cups (450g) dark chocolate Melts,
    melted
700g mixed fresh berries
150g white currants
1 bunch heart's ease

• ganache page 116

1   Grease deep 25cm round cake pan and deep 17cm round cake pan, line bases and sides with baking paper.

2   Beat butter and sugar in large bowl with electric mixer until light and fluffy. Add eggs, one at a time, beating until just combined between additions (mixture may curdle at this stage). Transfer mixture to larger bowl, stir in sifted flours, hazelnut meal, sour cream, raspberries and blackberries. Spread three-quarters of the mixture into 25cm prepared pan, spread remaining mixture into 17cm pan. Bake 25cm cake in moderate oven for about 1 3/4 hours. Bake 17cm cake in moderate oven about 1 hour. Stand cakes 5 minutes before turning onto wire racks to cool.

3   Centre 25cm cake, upside down, on plate.

4   Spread cake all over with about two-thirds of the ganache. Position 17cm cake, upside down, on 25cm cake; spread cake all over with remaining ganache.

5   Cut two strips of baking paper, one measuring 6.5cm x 55cm, the other 7.5cm x 80cm. Fold strips in half, then in half again; cut wave pattern 1cm from top. Spread smaller paper strip with one-third of the chocolate; wrap paper around 17cm cake, chocolate-side towards cake, and with ends overlapping at the back of the cake. Spread large paper strip with remaining chocolate; repeat process with 25cm cake. Leave about 10 minutes or until chocolate has set. Gently remove baking paper.

6   Decorate cake with fresh berries, currants and flowers.

tips  As an alternative, white chocolate Melts can be used instead of the dark for the collar. We used a 30cm glass stand for this cake, but a prepared 30cm round board can be used instead. Cake can be spread with ganache and decorated with chocolate bands 2 days ahead. Decorate cake with berries, currants and flowers 2 hours before required.

cut wave pattern from baking paper

spread chocolate over baking paper

gently remove baking paper

the decorated cake

# yuletide bombe-shell

3 litres vanilla ice-cream
410g jar fruit mince
2¹/₂ cups (375g) dark chocolate
   Melts, melted
1 bunch Christmas bush
1 bunch holly leaves
2 teaspoons icing sugar mixture

1 Line 1.75-litre (7-cup) pudding basin with plastic wrap, extending plastic about 5cm over edge of basin.

2 Place softened ice-cream and mince in large bowl, stir until combined. Spread ice-cream mixture into prepared pudding basin. Cover with lid or foil; freeze overnight.

3 Cut a piece of paper into 38cm circle to use as a guide. Cover paper with plastic wrap.

4 Turn ice-cream pudding onto tray, remove plastic wrap. Spread chocolate over plastic wrap. Quickly drape plastic, chocolate-side down, over pudding. Quickly smooth pudding with hands. Freeze until firm.

5 Gently peel away plastic.

6 Centre bombe on plate.

7 Just before serving, arrange Christmas bush and holly leaves around pudding; dust with sifted icing sugar.

tips Use egg slides to lift bombe onto plate. We used a 30cm glass stand for this cake, but a prepared 30cm round board can be used instead. The pudding must be made 1 day ahead, but can be made 1 week ahead; keep, covered, in freezer.

turn pudding onto tray

spread chocolate over plastic wrap

drape chocolate over pudding

smooth chocolate with hands

peel plastic from pudding

the decorated cake

# bundle of joy

Suitable cakes: fruit cake, page 100; chocolate mud cake, page 102; white chocolate mud cake, page 104.

3 x 23cm square cakes
1 cup (360g) apricot jam, warmed, strained, approximately
½ cup (80g) pure icing sugar, approximately
3.5kg prepared fondant
30cm square board
1 egg white, beaten lightly
1 cup (90g) desiccated coconut
1.5 metres cotton tape

- prepared fondant  page 113
- board  page 112
- patching  page 111
- covering cake  page 113

1   Select and make the cakes.

2   Level the tops of all the cakes so the cakes are the same height.

3   Reserve ½ cup (180g) of the jam. Sandwich all three cakes together with remaining jam.

4   On surface dusted with sifted icing sugar, knead prepared fondant until smooth; wrap fondant tightly in plastic wrap.

5   Centre cake on board. Brush cake all over with reserved jam. Patch and cover cake with fondant.

6   Using the side of your hand, mark five lines around sides of cake, at about 2cm intervals.

7   Brush cake all over with egg white. Sprinkle cake thickly with coconut.

8   Using blunt side of a table knife, mark in folds of the nappies around the sides of cake.

9   Secure tape around cake, tie bow.

tips  Cake can be completed 1 week ahead. Stick a large palette knife or egg slide between the cakes. Remove one cake at a time for cutting.

smooth fondant joins

use side of hand to mark cake

the marked fondant

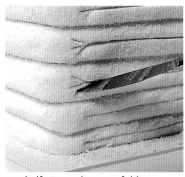
use knife to mark nappy folds

the decorated cake

*with love*

*This cake is classic simplicity... lovingly wrapped and tagged to suit any occasion*

# with love

Suitable cakes: fruit cake, page 100; chocolate mud cake, page 102; white chocolate mud cake, page 104.

23cm square cake
1/2 cup (80g) pure icing
    sugar, approximately
2kg prepared fondant
30cm square board
1 quantity sugar syrup
1 quantity modelling fondant
red and green colourings
cornflour
1/4 quantity royal icing
20cm x 2mm green ribbon
20cm x 2mm red ribbon

- prepared fondant  page 113
- board  page 112
- sugar syrup  page 110
- patching  page 111
- covering cake  page 113
- modelling fondant  page 115
- colourings  page 115
- royal icing  page 116
- piping bag  page 115

1  Select and make the cake.

2  Level the top of the cake if necessary.

3  On surface dusted with sifted icing sugar, knead prepared fondant until smooth; wrap tightly in plastic wrap.

4  Place cake, upside down, on board. Brush cake all over with sugar syrup. Patch and cover cake with fondant.

5  On surface dusted with sifted icing sugar, knead modelling fondant until smooth; reserve one-eighth of the fondant, wrap tightly in plastic wrap. Divide remaining fondant in half; knead red colouring into one half, wrap tightly in plastic wrap. Knead green colouring into other half of fondant, wrap tightly in plastic wrap.

6  On surface dusted with cornflour, roll reserved white fondant into 4cm x 8cm rectangle. Using small knife, trim edges to make a gift tag; use a skewer to make hole at top of tag. Place tag on tray lined with baking paper, allow to dry.

7  On surface dusted with cornflour, roll two-thirds of the red fondant into six 5cm logs; repeat with green fondant. Place logs side by side, alternating colours. On surface dusted with cornflour, roll logs into 18cm x 26cm rectangle. Using a ruler as a guide, trim edges; cut fondant into eight strips measuring 3cm x 17cm, cover with plastic wrap.

8  Cover a cardboard cylinder (from paper-towel roll) with baking paper. Wrap four fondant strips around cylinder, brush sugar syrup on inside of strips to secure ends together. Allow to dry.

9  Cut v-shape from ends of remaining strips; place on tray lined with baking paper, shape strips, allow to dry.

10 On surface dusted with cornflour, roll remaining red fondant into six 5cm logs, repeat with remaining green fondant. Place logs side by side, alternating colours, then roll logs into 13cm x 23cm rectangle. Using a ruler as a guide, trim edges; cut fondant into four strips measuring 3cm x 20cm. Brush one side of strip lightly with sugar syrup, attach to side and extend over top of cake, repeat with remaining strips. Using fondant scraps, roll into strip measuring 2cm x 5cm; attach ends together to make small cylinder, allow to dry.

11 Tint royal icing with green colouring. Place icing in piping bag fitted with small plain tube. Arrange dried fondant strips on top of cake to form bow, secure with a little of the icing.

12 Pipe message with icing on tag. Attach tag to bow with ribbons.

tips  Mix and match colours of ribbon to suit the occasion. Cake can be completed 1 week ahead.

cut fondant to form gift tag

alternate coloured fondant logs

roll fondant into rectangle

wrap fondant strips around cylinder

cut v-shape out of end of fondant strip

attach fondant strips to cake

# easter extravaganza

Suitable cake: butter cake, page 108.

2 x dolly varden cakes
1 quantity royal icing
½ cup (80g) pure icing sugar,
   approximately
2kg prepared fondant
30cm x 40cm oval board
1 quantity sugar syrup
green, lemon-yellow, sky-blue and
   pink colourings
1.3m x 4mm pink satin ribbon
1m pink feather boa

* royal icing  page 116
* prepared fondant  page 113
* board  page 112
* sugar syrup  page 110
* patching  page 111
* covering cake  page 113
* colourings  page 115
* securing ribbon  page 114
* piping bag  page 115

1 Make the cakes.

2 Level the tops of both cakes so the cakes are the same height.

3 Reserve half the royal icing in small bowl, cover tightly with plastic wrap. Sandwich cakes with remaining icing. Insert long wooden skewers at an angle through both cakes to secure, trim skewers level with surface of cake. Stand cake, supported in small bowl, about 1 hour or until icing is set.

4 Using sharp knife, trim both ends of cake to make an egg shape.

5 On surface dusted with sifted icing sugar, knead prepared fondant until smooth; wrap tightly in plastic wrap.

6 Centre cake on board. Brush cake all over with sugar syrup. Patch and cover cake with fondant.

7 Divide reserved royal icing evenly into four small bowls. Using colourings, tint icing green, yellow, blue and pink, cover tightly with plastic wrap.

8 Secure ribbon around centre of cake with a little icing. Place green icing into piping bag fitted with small plain tube, pipe heart pattern between ribbons; reserve icing.

9 Place yellow icing into piping bag fitted with small plain tube, pipe daisy pattern along both sides of ribbon. Pipe dots of green icing in centre of daisies. Place blue icing into piping bag fitted with small plain tube, pipe flower pattern on either side of daisy pattern.

10 Place pink icing into piping bag fitted with small plain tube. Pipe outline for cornelli pattern on both ends of cake, fill in with cornelli pattern.

11 Place feather boa around cake.

tips A dolly varden cake tin can be purchased from cookware shops or cake decorating suppliers. A pudding basin can be substituted, however the cakes will probably need more trimming. Cake can be completed 2 days ahead. Remove skewers when cutting the cake.

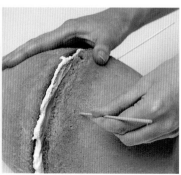
secure cakes with skewers

trim ends of cake to make egg shape

pipe hearts onto cake

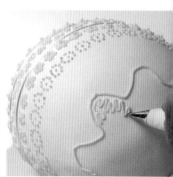
pipe cornelli pattern

# masquerade

Suitable cakes: chocolate mud cake, page 102; white chocolate mud cake, page 104; carrot cake, page 106; butter cake, page 108.

28cm x 34cm rectangle cake
30cm x 40cm oval board
1 quantity vienna cream
sky-blue and royal-blue colourings
1/4 cup (40g) pure icing sugar,
    approximately
500g prepared fondant
1 egg white
1/3 cup (75g) blue sugar
black colouring
1/2 quantity royal icing
60 x 1.5cm blue diamantés
26 x 1cm blue diamantés
covered 20-gauge wire
8 blue feathers, approximately

* template  page 94
* board  page 112
* vienna cream page 116
* colourings  page 115
* prepared fondant  page 113
* coloured sugar  page 114
* royal icing  page 116
* piping bag  page 115

1  Select and make the cake.

2  Level the top of the cake if necessary.

3  Cut cake using mask template as a guide.

4  Centre cake, upside down, on board.

5  Tint vienna cream using sky-blue and royal-blue colourings. Spread cake all over with cream.

6  On surface dusted with sifted icing sugar, knead prepared fondant until smooth. Knead sky-blue and royal-blue colourings into fondant; wrap tightly in plastic wrap.

7  Roll fondant onto surface dusted with sifted icing sugar until large enough to cut out mask shape. Cut out mask using template as a guide. Using a skewer, mark eyes onto fondant. Gently lift fondant onto cake.

8  Brush egg white around eyes, sprinkle around eyes with coloured sugar.

9  Paint eyes with black colouring.

10 Place royal icing into piping bag. Pipe small dots of icing onto back of large diamantés, attach to cake to define mask. Repeat process with small diamantés to define eyes.

11 Sew pieces of wire to back of feathers. Arrange feathers on top of cake.

tips  To serve cake, either remove all non-edible diamantés and feathers or lift fondant mask off cake. Cake can be completed 2 days ahead.

cut out cake using template

use a skewer to mark eyes

brush egg white around eyes

sew wires to back of feathers

the decorated cake

*summer frost*

*sophisticated and cool... who would have thought a frost in summer could be so appealing?*

# summer frost

6 eggs
1 cup (220g) caster sugar
1/2 cup (75g) plain flour
1/2 cup (75g) self-raising flour
1/2 cup (75g) cornflour
2m x 5cm white checked
    organza ribbon
150g cherries
1 cup (175g) white grapes
2 small Kaffir limes, quartered
6 Kaffir lime leaves
2 egg whites, beaten lightly
1 cup (220g) caster sugar, extra
2 glacé clementines, quartered

PASSIONFRUIT CURD

4 eggs
3/4 cup (165g) caster sugar
1/2 cup (125ml) passionfruit pulp
1/4 cup (60ml) water
2 teaspoons finely grated
    lemon rind
125g butter, chopped

MERINGUE

2/3 cup (160ml) water
1 1/4 cups (275g) caster sugar
4 egg whites

1  Grease two deep 22cm round cake pans, line bases with baking paper.

2  Beat eggs and sugar in medium bowl with electric mixer about 10 minutes or until thick and sugar is dissolved. Transfer mixture to large bowl.

3  Gently fold one-third of triple-sifted flours into egg mixture, then fold in remaining flours. Divide mixture evenly between pans. Bake in moderate oven about 20 minutes or until cooked when tested. Turn cakes onto wire racks to cool.

4  Split cakes in half. Place bottom layer of one cake on oven tray. Reserve 1 cup (250ml) Passionfruit Curd in small bowl. Spread cake layer with one-third of the remaining curd, top with another cake layer. Spread with half of the remaining curd, top with another cake layer. Spread with remaining curd and top with remaining cake layer. Spread cake all over with reserved curd.

5  Spread cake all over with Meringue. Bake in moderately hot oven about 3 minutes or until meringue is lightly browned.

6  Centre cake on plate.

7  Secure ribbon around cake.

8  Brush cherries, grapes, limes and leaves individually with egg white; dip wet fruit and leaves in extra sugar. Place frosted fruit and leaves on tray lined with baking paper. Leave about 1 hour or until sugar is dry.

9  Arrange fruit and leaves on cake.

Passionfruit Curd  Combine ingredients in medium heatproof bowl over simmering water; stir until mixture thickly coats wooden spoon. Cover, cool; refrigerate.

Meringue  Combine the water and 1 cup (220g) of the sugar in small saucepan; stir over heat, without boiling, until sugar is dissolved. Boil, uncovered, without stirring, until syrup reaches 116°C on candy thermometer, or when a teaspoon of syrup, dropped into a cup of cold water, will form a soft ball when rolled between fingers. Remove from heat to allow bubbles to subside. Meanwhile, beat egg whites in small bowl with electric mixer on high speed until soft peaks form; add remaining sugar, beat until dissolved. While mixer is operating, add hot syrup in thin stream; beat on high speed about 10 minutes or until mixture is thick and cool.

tips  We used a 30cm glass stand for this cake, but a prepared 30cm round board can be used instead. You may need to vary the fruit you use depending on season and availability. The sponge cake can be made 1 month ahead and frozen. Passionfruit curd can be made 2 weeks ahead; keep covered in refrigerator. Assemble cake and complete 3 hours ahead.

...ed flours into egg mixture

stir passionfruit curd until thick

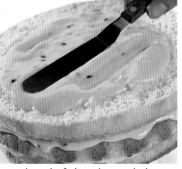
spread passionfruit curd over cake layer

brush egg white onto fruit, dip into sugar

# tiffany sweetheart cake

Suitable cakes: chocolate mud cake, page 102; white chocolate mud cake, page 104;
carrot cake, page 106; butter cake, page 108.

28cm x 34cm rectangle cake
23cm square cake
1 tablespoon pure icing sugar,
   approximately
300g modelling fondant
rose-pink colouring
cornflour
2.5cm heart-shaped cutter
2 quantities fluffy frosting
delphinium-blue colouring
41cm x 51cm heart-shaped board
13g packet silver cachous

- template  page 94
- modelling fondant  page 115
- colourings  page 115
- fluffy frosting  page 117
- board  page 112

1 Select and make the cakes.

2 Level the cakes so the cakes are the same height.

3 Cut cakes using heart template as a guide.

4 On a surface dusted with sifted icing sugar, knead modelling fondant
until smooth. Reserve half the fondant; wrap tightly in plastic wrap. Knead
pink colouring into remaining fondant; wrap tightly in plastic wrap.
On surface dusted with cornflour, roll white fondant to approximately
2mm thick. Cut out heart shapes using cutter; cover remaining fondant
with plastic wrap to prevent drying. Using cornfloured fingers, pinch
sharp end of heart and bend tops in slightly, leave to dry on tray lined
with baking paper. Repeat process with remaining white and pink fondant.

5 Tint fluffy frosting pink using pink and blue colourings.

6 Centre cake, upside down, on board. Spread cake all over with frosting.

7 Arrange hearts and cachous on cake.

tips Fluffy frosting will set like a meringue. Cake can be completed
2 days ahead, but frosting will lose its gloss.

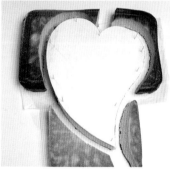
cut out cakes using template

cut out hearts from modelling fondant

shape hearts with fingers

spread frosting over cake

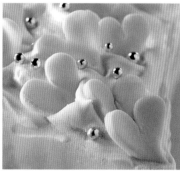
the decorated cake in close-up

# fanned chocolate torte

250g butter, chopped
1/4 cup (60ml) dark rum
2 tablespoons dry instant coffee
1 1/4 cups (310ml) water
200g dark chocolate, chopped
2 cups (440g) caster sugar
1 1/2 cups (225g) self-raising flour
1 cup (150g) plain flour
1/4 cup (25g) cocoa powder
2 eggs
1 quantity dark chocolate ganache
400g dark chocolate, melted, extra
1 tablespoon cocoa powder, extra

• ganache page 116

1 Grease deep 22cm round cake pan, line base and side with baking paper.

2 Combine butter, rum, coffee and the water in medium saucepan; stir over heat until butter is melted. Bring to a boil, remove from heat; add chocolate and sugar, stir until chocolate is melted and sugar dissolved. Cool 5 minutes.

3 Sift flours and cocoa into large bowl; gradually whisk in chocolate mixture and eggs.

4 Pour mixture into prepared pan; bake in slow oven about 1 hour 40 minutes, covering halfway through cooking. Stand 5 minutes before turning onto wire rack to cool.

5 Split cake into three equal layers. Sandwich layers with one-third of the ganache. Centre cake on plate. Spread cake all over with remaining ganache.

6 Using baking paper, cut out three circles, measuring 12cm, 16cm and 23cm. Cut each circle into quarters. Spread extra chocolate evenly over the pieces of baking paper. Drape chocolate over 1cm-diameter foil-covered candles to create a corrugated effect; leave about 5 minutes or until set. Gently remove baking paper.

7 Position chocolate frills on cake; dust cake with sifted extra cocoa.

tips We used a 30cm glass stand for this cake, but a prepared 30cm round board can be used instead. Cake can be completed 2 days ahead; cover, refrigerate.

spread chocolate onto baking paper

shape chocolate over candles

the decorated cake

# marbled christening special

Suitable cakes: fruit cake, page 100; chocolate mud cake, page 102;
white chocolate mud cake, page 104; carrot cake, page 106; butter cake, page 108.

24cm x 32cm oval cake
1/2 cup (80g) pure icing sugar,
    approximately
2kg prepared fondant
rose-pink colouring
30cm x 38cm oval board
1 quantity sugar syrup
1.5m x 3.5cm pink satin ribbon
1m x 7mm pink satin ribbon
pink daisies

• prepared fondant  page 113
• colourings  page 115
• board  page 112
• sugar syrup  page 110
• patching  page 111
• covering cake  page 113
• securing ribbon  page 111

1  Select and make the cake.

2  Level the top of the cake if necessary.

3  On surface dusted with sifted icing sugar, knead prepared fondant
   until smooth. Gently knead pink colouring into fondant until colour is
   marbled. Wrap fondant tightly in plastic wrap.

4  Centre cake, upside down, on board. Brush cake all over with sugar
   syrup. Patch and cover cake with fondant.

5  Secure 3.5cm-wide ribbon around cake.

6  Reserve 40cm of the 7mm ribbon. Using pointed vegetable knife,
   make small incisions into cake 2cm apart, about 2cm from edge of
   cake. Cut 7mm-wide ribbon into 3cm lengths. Insert ribbon into
   incisions using tweezers.

7  Arrange flowers and reserved ribbon on top of cake.

   tips  It is important to insert ribbon in fondant before it becomes firm.
   Helleborus (Winter Rose) can be used as a substitute for daisies. We used
   fresh daisies for this cake, but artificial flowers are also suitable. Cake can be
   completed (without flowers) 1 week ahead. Position fresh flowers on cake 1
   hour ahead.

marbling fondant

rolling fondant to cover cake

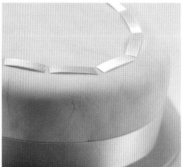

secure ribbon around cake

insert ribbon into cake

the decorated cake

# cake by candlelight

Suitable cakes: carrot cake, page 106; butter cake, page 108.

2 x 8cm-x-17cm nut roll cakes
2cm round cutter
1.25kg (8 cups) icing sugar mixture
2 tablespoons vegetable oil
²/₃ cup (160ml) milk, approximately
2 cups (180g) desiccated coconut
33cm round board
3 x 2cm-diameter white candles

• board  page 112

1 Select and make the cakes.

2 Cut top off one cake at an angle. Cut one-third off remaining cake at an angle.

3 Using cutter, cut a small hole out of top of all three cakes.

4 Place icing sugar in large heatproof bowl, stir in oil and enough milk to make a soft paste. Place bowl over a saucepan of simmering water, stir until icing is pourable. Reserve one-quarter of the icing in small jug, cover tightly with plastic wrap. Place remaining icing in medium jug.

5 Stand cakes on wire rack over tray. Pour about half the icing evenly over cakes; stand 2 minutes or until icing is partly set. Pour remaining icing over cakes for a second layer.

6 Place coconut onto another tray. Insert a skewer through centre of each cake then, before icing sets, roll cakes in coconut.

7 Position cakes on board.

8 Cut candles into 3cm lengths; wrap ends of candles in foil. Place candles in holes in cakes.

9 Drizzle reserved icing over cakes to represent melted candle wax.

tips  This cake is great as a centrepiece on your Christmas table.
Cake can be completed 1 day ahead.

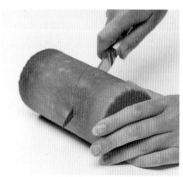
cut one cake at an angle

use cutter to make holes in cakes

pour icing over cakes

roll cake in coconut

place foil-wrapped candles into cakes

the decorated cake

# christmas bauble

Suitable cakes: fruit cake, page 100; butter cake, page 108.

2 x 9-cup pudding basin cakes
1/2 cup (80g) pure icing sugar,
   approximately
1.5kg prepared fondant
3/4 cup (270g) apricot jam, warmed,
   strained, approximately
1 tablespoon cornflour,
   approximately
gold lustre colour
silver lustre colour
1 quantity royal icing
3 x 13g packets gold cachous
2m x 2.5cm gold and silver
   organza ribbon
covered 24-gauge wire

• prepared fondant  page 113
• patching  page 111
• covering cake  page 113
• colourings  page 115
• royal icing  page 116
• piping bag  page 115

1  Select and make the cakes.

2  Level the tops of both cakes so the cakes are the same height.

3  On surface dusted with sifted icing sugar, knead prepared fondant until smooth; wrap fondant tightly in plastic wrap.

4  Sandwich cakes with jam. Brush cake all over with jam. Patch and cover cake with half the fondant.

5  Sift cornflour evenly over the fondant. Brush a 3cm band of jam around base of cake, to secure the second layer of fondant. Cover cake with remaining fondant.

6  Centre cake on plate.

7  Using the blunt edge of a small knife, gently mark cake into six segments.

8  Brush gold and silver lustre colouring onto cakes.

9  Place royal icing into piping bag fitted with small plain tube. Pipe icing along segments, a little at a time; using tweezers, position cachous on icing before it sets.

10 Make bow with ribbon, secure with wire; attach to top of cake.

tips Gold and silver colourings are not edible, so we gave this cake two layers of fondant so the painted layer can be removed and discarded. We used a 30cm glass stand for this cake, but a prepared 30cm round board can be used instead. Cake can be completed 2 days ahead.

sandwich cakes with jam

brush lustre onto segments

define segments with cachous

the decorated cake

# tulips in spring

this quirky tower of tulips says 'I love you' in a delightfully unexpected way

# *tulips in spring*

Suitable cakes: chocolate mud cake, page 102; white chocolate mud cake, page 104; butter cake, page 108.

2 x 15cm round cakes
2 x 12cm round cakes
1 quantity vienna cream
6 cups (900g) white chocolate
   Melts, melted
1m x 5cm wired checked ribbon
10 orange tulips
florist tape
covered 24-gauge wire

- vienna cream  page 116
- piping bag  page 115
- florist tape  page 114

1  Select and make the cakes.

2  Level the tops of all cakes so the cakes are the same height.

3  Sandwich 15cm cakes with a little of the vienna cream. Centre cake on plate. Spread cake all over with half the cream. Sandwich 12cm cakes with more cream; centre cake on top of 15cm cake, spread cake all over with remaining cream.

4  Cut baking paper into two sheets measuring 15cm x 60cm and two sheets measuring 10cm x 60cm. Reserve $1/2$ cup (75g) of the chocolate in small bowl. Spread one-quarter of the remaining chocolate evenly over one of the sheets of baking paper, repeat process with remaining chocolate and paper; lift pieces of paper to allow excess chocolate to drip from the edges. Leave chocolate about 5 minutes or until almost set. Gently remove baking paper. Using a sharp knife and a ruler as a guide, cut chocolate into 4cm panels.

5  Place reserved chocolate into piping bag, pipe hearts onto half the chocolate panels.

6  Overlap chocolate panels around side of cake.

7  Secure ribbon around cake with a little piped chocolate.

8  Bind ends of flowers with florist tape. Insert end of wire into top of flower, twist wire around stem for support.

9  Gently push flowers into cake.

tips Gerberas may be used as an alternative to tulips. We used a 30cm glass stand for this cake, but a prepared 30cm round board can be used instead. Cake can be completed (without flowers) 2 days ahead. Position flowers 2 hours ahead.

spread chocolate over baking paper

lift paper to neaten chocolate edges

cut chocolate into 4cm panels

pipe hearts onto chocolate

position chocolate panels around cake

bind ends of flowers with florist tape

twist wire around stems of flowers

# templates

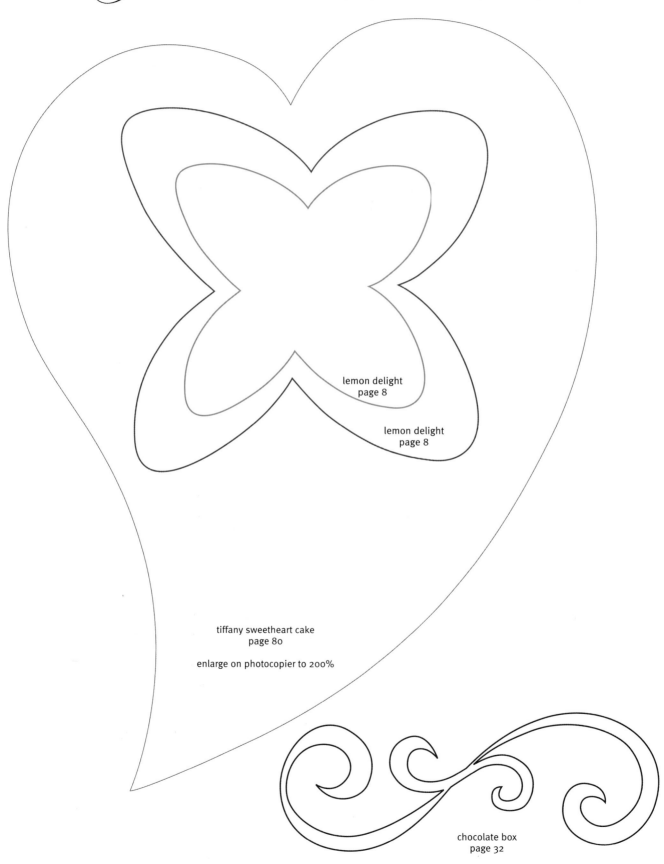

lemon delight
page 8

lemon delight
page 8

tiffany sweetheart cake
page 80

enlarge on photocopier to 200%

chocolate box
page 32

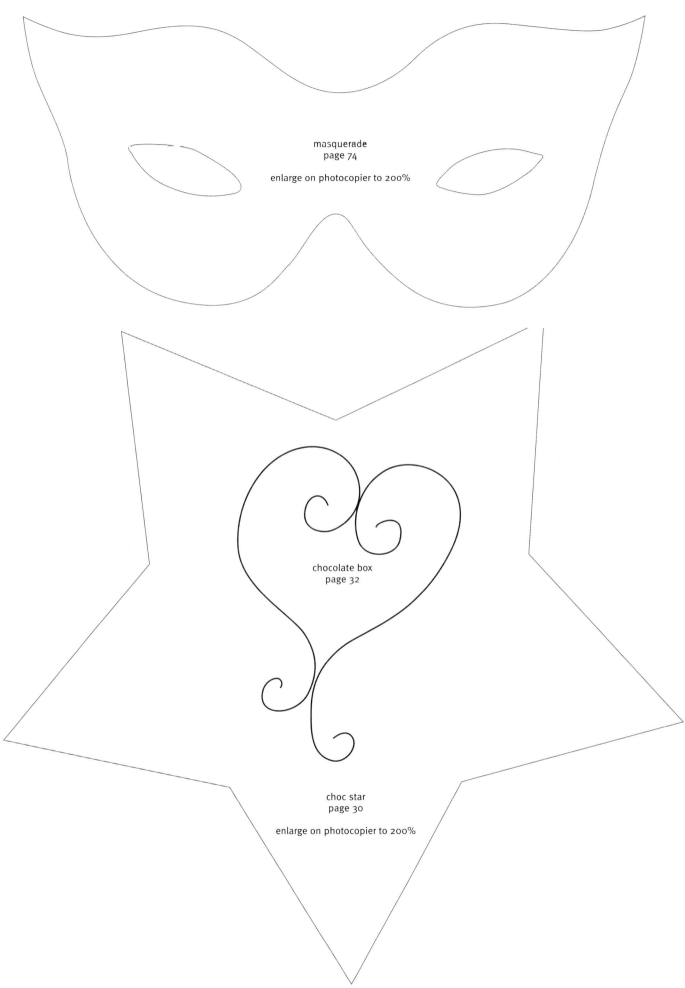

masquerade
page 74

enlarge on photocopier to 200%

chocolate box
page 32

choc star
page 30

enlarge on photocopier to 200%

basic know-how

# getting started

From leafing through this book, you've no doubt developed a pretty clear picture of the variety, size and shape of the cake you'd like to make. Now for the practicalities. It's not hard to achieve professional-looking results provided you allow time to read the instructions on these, and the following, information pages. Then follow the recipes without omitting any steps. The quality of the completed cake depends on correctly laid foundations.

## cake pans

Each recipe specifies the required sizes of cake pans and the necessary quantities to make your cakes look the same as ours – however, cake sizes and shapes can be changed to suit yourself and your chosen decorations.

Use well-shaped, rigid, straight-sided, deep cake pans. The ones we used are made from good-quality tin or aluminium.

We used cake pans bought from cookware stores and shops specialising in cake decorating equipment.

coming up daisies, page 22

snip paper at base of all shapes of cake pan, to fit paper neatly into pan

cut paper to cover base; repeat lining process with greaseproof or baking paper

### TO LINE CAKE PANS

Lining a cake pan neatly minimises time-consuming trimming and patching of cakes.

The lining helps to protect the cake during baking. For fruit cakes, use one sheet of strong brown paper and two sheets of baking or greaseproof paper. Cut paper at base of pan at an angle, so that paper fits corners neatly.

cut a pattern from greaseproof or baking paper; secure to cake with toothpicks

some unusually shaped cake pans; all these shapes can be cut from round cakes

### UNUSUAL SHAPES IN CAKES

We used bought cake pans, however, cakes of an unusual shape, such as a heart, an oval, an octagon or even a petal, can all be cut from round cakes.

From a square cake you can easily cut a cake into diamond or rectangular shapes.

# tiered cakes

There are several ways to make tiered cakes. Cakes can be placed directly on top of each other, although some cakes need to be supported with skewers. This is especially necessary when heavy fruit cakes are used. Wooden skewers bought from butchers or craft shops are ideal – these are inserted in the lower tier/s of cakes, under the area that the upper tier will cover; the size of the board on the upper tier/s should be used as a guide when positioning the skewers.

You will need three or four skewers to support the upper tier/s. Insert the skewers, pointed-end first, in the correct position, through the icing and the cake, right down to the board. Withdraw the skewers and insert them, blunt-end first, into the holes. Mark the skewers level with the surface of the cake, noting the position of each skewer; withdraw the skewers and cut them off at the marks. Insert the skewers back into the cake, ready to support the upper tier.

push pointed end of skewers into cake, remove; push blunt ends into cake

mark skewers close to surface of cake; note position of each skewer

# how to transport cakes

Cakes can be transported easily by placing them on a piece of thin sponge rubber (to prevent slipping) in a box as close to the size of the board as possible. Cover an open box with clear plastic, sit box flat.

Tiered cakes are always transported with the tiers separated, and then assembled when they reach their destination.

# to cut a wedding cake

As a guide, a 25cm square cake can be cut into 100 finger-length pieces. Cut a round cake crossways into slices before cutting into finger-length pieces.

use sharp serrated knife to cut skewers at marks; use sandpaper to smooth ends

# to store a cooked fruit cake

When the cake is cold, remove from the pan. Discard brown paper, leave inner lining paper intact. Wrap cake tightly in plastic wrap to keep airtight, then in foil or tea-towels to keep the light out. Store in a cool dark place. If in doubt about hot or humid weather, store the cake in the refrigerator.

The cake will keep for 1 year at room temperature if cooked and stored correctly; it can be frozen indefinitely if preferred.

replace skewers in original positions; these skewers support the next tier

# to store a decorated fruit cake

Cakes will keep well if they have been correctly covered with almond icing and fondant. They need to be protected from moisture in the air, either rain or humidity or, worse, both. If possible, keep the cake in a cabinet or under glass or plastic so you can check for changes in the cake's appearance.

If the surface of the cake becomes wet and sticky, remove the cake from the cabinet and stand it under an ordinary reading lamp (not fluorescent). Turn the cake every now and then until the fondant looks and feels dry, then return it to the cabinet.

Decorated cakes can be frozen if they are to be kept for more than 3 months. Thaw the cake, covered, in the refrigerator. This process will take approximately 2 days.

# rich fruit cake

| INGREDIENTS | 15cm round | 17cm round<br>15cm square<br>17cm octagonal | 20cm round<br>9-cup pudding basin | 22cm round<br>19cm square |
|---|---|---|---|---|
| raisins, chopped | 125g | 160g | 200g | 250g |
| glacé cherries, quartered | 60g | 90g | 100g | 125g |
| sultanas | 375g | 560g | 600g | 750g |
| dried currants | 60g | 90g | 100g | 125g |
| mixed peel | 60g | 90g | 100g | 125g |
| marmalade | 1 tbs | 1$\frac{1}{2}$ tbs | 1$\frac{1}{2}$ tbs | 2 tbs |
| dark rum | $\frac{1}{4}$ cup | $\frac{1}{3}$ cup | $\frac{1}{3}$ cup | $\frac{1}{2}$ cup |
| butter * | 125g | 160g | 200g | 250g |
| finely grated orange rind | $\frac{1}{2}$ tsp | $\frac{3}{4}$ tsp | $\frac{3}{4}$ tsp | 1 tsp |
| finely grated lemon rind | $\frac{1}{2}$ tsp | $\frac{3}{4}$ tsp | $\frac{3}{4}$ tsp | 1 tsp |
| brown sugar** | $\frac{1}{2}$ cup | $\frac{3}{4}$ cup | $\frac{3}{4}$ cup | 1 cup |
| eggs* | 2 | 3 | 3 | 4 |
| plain flour | 1 cup | 1$\frac{1}{2}$ cups | 1$\frac{2}{3}$ cups | 2 cups |
| mixed spice | $\frac{1}{2}$ tsp | $\frac{3}{4}$ tsp | 1 tsp | 1 tsp |
| baking time | 2$\frac{1}{2}$ hours | 2$\frac{1}{2}$ to 3$\frac{1}{2}$ hours | 3 hours | 3 to 3$\frac{1}{2}$ hours |

all cake pans must be deep and straight-sided (not sloping) except for the pudding basin
* butter and eggs should be at room temperature for best results   ** brown sugar should be firmly packed into measuring cup

push spoonfuls of mixture into edge of cake pan

feel blade of knife to determine if cake is cooked

turn hot cake, upside down, onto foil

| 25cm round 23cm square | 28cm round 30cm heart 26cm octagonal | 30cm round 28cm square | 30cm square | 24cm x 32cm oval |
|---|---|---|---|---|
| 375g | 500g | 625g | 750g | 460g |
| 185g | 250g | 315g | 375g | 230g |
| 1kg | 1.125kg | 1.75kg | 2kg | 1kg |
| 185g | 250g | 315g | 375g | 230g |
| 185g | 250g | 315g | 375g | 230g |
| 1/4 cup | 1/3 cup | 5 tbs | 1/2 cup | 1/4 cup |
| 3/4 cup | 1 cup | 1¼ cups | 1½ cups | 3/4 cup |
| 375g | 500g | 625g | 750g | 460g |
| 1 tsp | 2 tsp | 2 tsp | 3 tsp | 1 tsp |
| 1 tsp | 2 tsp | 2 tsp | 3 tsp | 1 tsp |
| 1½ cups | 2 cups | 2½ cups | 3 cups | 1¾ cups |
| 6 | 8 | 10 | 12 | 7 |
| 3 cups | 4 cups | 5 cups | 6 cups | 3¾ cups |
| 1½ tsp | 2 tsp | 2½ tsp | 3 tsp | 1 tsp |
| 4 hours | 5 to 5½ hours | 6 to 6½ hours | 6 to 7 hours | 4½ hours |

1  Line base and sides of cake pan with one layer of brown paper and two layers of greaseproof or baking paper; bring paper 5cm above edge of pan.

2  Mix fruit, marmalade and rum in large bowl. Beat butter, rinds and sugar in bowl with electric mixer until just combined; beat in eggs, one at a time, until just combined between additions. Stir butter mixture into fruit mixture; mix in sifted flour and spice. Spread mixture into the prepared pan. Tap pan on bench to settle mixture into pan. Level top of cake with wet spatula.

3  Bake in slow oven for time given in chart.

4  Feel surface of cake; it should be firm. Remove cake from oven, close oven door, gently push blade of a sharp-pointed vegetable knife straight through centre of cake, right to base of pan. Withdraw knife slowly, feel blade with your fingers. If you feel uncooked mixture, return cake to oven for another 15 minutes before testing again. If blade is free from mixture, the cake is cooked through.

5  Immediately the cake is cooked, cut off paper around edge of pan. Turn cake upside down onto foil; wrap cake and pan tightly in foil. Cooling cake upside down will make cake sit flat and level for decorating.

# chocolate mud cake

| INGREDIENTS | 12cm round | 15cm round | 17cm round<br>15cm square<br>17cm octagonal | 20cm round | 22cm round<br>19cm square |
|---|---|---|---|---|---|
| dark chocolate | 185g | 270g | 360g | 625g | 675g |
| butter | 125g | 175g | 225g | 395g | 430g |
| dry instant coffee | 2 tsp | 3 tsp | 1 tbs | $1^1/_2$ tbs | $1^1/_2$ tbs |
| water | $^1/_3$ cup | $^1/_2$ cup | $^3/_4$ cup | 1 cup | $1^1/_4$ cups |
| brown sugar* | $^1/_3$ cup | $^1/_2$ cup | $^3/_4$ cup | 1 cup | $1^1/_4$ cups |
| plain flour | $^1/_2$ cup | $^3/_4$ cup | 1 cup | $1^1/_2$ cups | $1^3/_4$ cups |
| SR flour | 2 tbs | $^1/_4$ cup | $^1/_4$ cup | $^1/_3$ cup | $^1/_2$ cup |
| eggs | 1 | 1 | 2 | 3 | 4 |
| coffee liqueur | 2 tbs | $^1/_4$ cup | $^1/_4$ cup | $^1/_3$ cup | $^1/_3$ cup |
| baking time | $1^1/_2$ hours | $1^3/_4$ hours | 2 hours | $2^1/_4$ hours | $2^1/_2$ hours |

all cake pans must be deep and straight-sided (not sloping)
* brown sugar should be firmly packed into measuring cup

pour cake mixture into prepared pan

| 25cm round<br>23cm square | 28cm round<br>30cm heart<br>28cm x 34cm baking dish<br>26cm octagonal | 30cm round<br>28cm square | 30cm square | 24cm x 32cm oval |
|---|---|---|---|---|
| 840g | 1.25kg | 1.45kg | 1.68kg | 1kg |
| 525g | 750g | 900g | 1kg | 650g |
| 2 tbs | $^1/_4$ cup | $^1/_3$ cup | $^1/_3$ cup | $2^1/_2$ tbs |
| $1^1/_2$ cups | $2^1/_4$ cups | $2^2/_3$ cups | 3 cups | $1^3/_4$ cups |
| $1^1/_2$ cups | $2^1/_4$ cups | $2^2/_3$ cups | 3 cups | $1^3/_4$ cups |
| 2 cups | 3 cups | $3^1/_2$ cups | 4 cups | $2^1/_3$ cups |
| $^1/_2$ cup | $^3/_4$ cup | 1 cup | 1 cup | $^2/_3$ cup |
| 4 | 6 | 7 | 8 | 5 |
| $^1/_2$ cup | $^3/_4$ cup | 1 cup | 1 cup | $^2/_3$ cup |
| 3 hours | $3^1/_2$ hours | 4 hours | $4^1/_2$ hours | $3^1/_4$ hours |

1  Grease and line base and sides of cake pan with one thickness of baking paper, bringing paper 5cm above side of pan.

2  Combine chopped chocolate, chopped butter, coffee, water and sugar in saucepan; stir over low heat until chocolate is melted and sugar dissolved. Transfer mixture to a bowl; cool 15 minutes.

3  Stir in sifted flours, lightly beaten eggs and liqueur. Pour mixture into prepared pan.

4  Bake in moderately slow oven for time given in chart. Cover cake with foil halfway through baking if cake is becoming dark and crusty.

5  Cake will develop a thick sugary crust during baking; test for firmness by touching with fingers about 5 minutes before end of baking time. Then, test with skewer.

6  Cool cake in pan.

tip  The cake will keep well for 1 week in an airtight container; or, it can be frozen for 3 months.

feel crust of cake for firmness; cracks are normal

insert skewer into cake to determine if it is cooked

# white chocolate mud cake

| INGREDIENTS | 12cm round | 15cm round | 17cm round<br>15cm square<br>17cm octagonal | 20cm round | 22cm round<br>19cm square |
|---|---|---|---|---|---|
| unsalted butter | 85g | 125g | 165g | 250g | 335g |
| white chocolate | 45g | 75g | 100g | 150g | 200g |
| caster sugar | $^2/_3$ cup | 1 cup | $1^1/_3$ cups | 2 cups | $2^2/_3$ cups |
| milk | $^1/_3$ cup | $^1/_2$ cup | $^2/_3$ cup | 1 cup | $1^1/_2$ cups |
| plain flour | $^1/_2$ cup | $^3/_4$ cup | 1 cup | $1^1/_2$ cups | 2 cups |
| SR flour | 2 tbs | $^1/_4$ cup | $^1/_3$ cup | $^1/_2$ cup | $^2/_3$ cup |
| vanilla essence | $^1/_4$ tsp | $^1/_2$ tsp | $^1/_2$ tsp | 1 tsp | 1 tsp |
| eggs | 1 | 1 | 1 | 2 | 3 |
| baking time | 1 hour | $1^1/_2$ hours | $1^3/_4$ hours | $1^3/_4$ hours | 2 hours |

all cake pans must be deep and straight-sided (not sloping)

pour cake mixture into prepared pan

| 25cm round<br>23cm square | 28cm round<br>30cm heart<br>28cm x 34cm baking dish<br>26cm octagonal | 30cm round<br>28cm square | 30cm square | 24cm x 32cm oval |
| --- | --- | --- | --- | --- |
| 375g | 500g | 625g | 750g | 460g |
| 225g | 300g | 375g | 450g | 270g |
| 3 cups | 4 cups | 5 cups | 6 cups | $3^2/_3$ cups |
| $1^1/_2$ cups | 2 cups | $2^1/_2$ cups | 3 cups | $1^3/_4$ cups |
| $2^1/_4$ cups | 3 cups | $3^3/_4$ cups | $4^1/_2$ cups | $2^3/_4$ cups |
| $3/_4$ cup | 1 cup | $1^1/_4$ cups | $1^1/_2$ cups | 1 cup |
| $1^1/_2$ tsp | 2 tsp | $2^1/_2$ tsp | 3 tsp | 2 tsp |
| 3 | 4 | 5 | 6 | 4 |
| $2^1/_2$ hours | 3 hours | $3^1/_2$ hours | 4 hours | 3 hours |

feel crust of cake for firmness; cracks are normal

insert skewer into cake to determine if it is cooked

1 Grease and line base and sides of cake pan with one thickness of baking paper, bringing paper 5cm above side of pan.

2 Combine chopped butter, chopped chocolate, sugar and milk in saucepan; stir over low heat until chocolate is melted and sugar dissolved. Transfer mixture to a bowl; cool 15 minutes.

3 Stir in sifted flours, essence and lightly beaten eggs. Pour mixture into prepared pan.

4 Bake in moderately slow oven for time given in chart. Cover cake with foil halfway through baking if cake is over-browning.

5 Cake will develop a thick sugary crust during baking; test for firmness by touching with fingers about 5 minutes before the end of baking time. Then, test with skewer.

6 Cool cake in pan.

tip The cake will keep well for 1 week in an airtight container; or, it can be frozen for 3 months.

# carrot cake

| INGREDIENTS | 12cm round | 15cm round<br>8cm x 17cm nut roll tin | 17cm round<br>15cm square | 20cm round | 22cm round<br>19cm square |
|---|---|---|---|---|---|
| SR flour | 1/3 cup | 1/2 cup | 3/4 cup | 1 cup | 1 1/2 cups |
| plain flour | 1/4 cup | 1/3 cup | 1/2 cup | 2/3 cup | 1 cup |
| bicarb soda | 1/4 tsp | 1/2 tsp | 1/2 tsp | 3/4 tsp | 1 tsp |
| cinnamon | 1/2 tsp | 1/2 tsp | 1 tsp | 1 1/2 tsp | 2 tsp |
| nutmeg | 1/2 tsp | 1/2 tsp | 1 tsp | 1 1/2 tsp | 2 tsp |
| brown sugar* | 1/4 cup | 1/3 cup | 1/2 cup | 2/3 cup | 1 cup |
| coarsely grated carrot* | 3/4 cup | 1 cup | 1 1/2 cups | 2 cups | 3 cups |
| vegetable oil | 1/4 cup | 1/3 cup | 1/2 cup | 2/3 cup | 1 cup |
| eggs | 1 | 1 | 2 | 3 | 4 |
| sour cream | 1/4 cup | 1/3 cup | 1/2 cup | 2/3 cup | 1 cup |
| baking time | 50 minutes | 1 hour | 1 1/4 hours | 1 1/2 hours | 1 3/4 hours |

all cake pans must be deep and straight-sided (not sloping)
* brown sugar and carrot should be firmly packed into measuring cup

spread cake mixture into prepared cake pan

insert skewer into cake to determine if it is cooked

turn cake onto rack; use second rack to invert cake

| 25cm round<br>23cm square | 28cm round<br>30cm heart<br>28cm x 34cm baking dish<br>26cm octagonal | 30cm round<br>28cm square | 30cm square | 24cm x 32cm oval |
|---|---|---|---|---|
| 1³/₄ cups | 2¹/₄ cups | 3 cups | 3³/₄ cups | 2³/₄ cups |
| 1¹/₄ cups | 1¹/₂ cups | 2 cups | 2¹/₂ cups | 1³/₄ cups |
| 1¹/₄ tsp | 1¹/₂ tsp | 2 tsp | 2¹/₂ tsp | 1³/₄ tsp |
| 2¹/₂ tsp | 3 tsp | 1 tbs | 1¹/₄ tbs | 3 tsp |
| 2¹/₂ tsp | 3 tsp | 1 tbs | 1¹/₄ tbs | 3 tsp |
| 1¹/₄ cups | 1¹/₂ cups | 2 cups | 2¹/₂ cups | 1³/₄ cups |
| 3³/₄ cups | 4¹/₂ cups | 6 cups | 7¹/₂ cups | 5¹/₄ cups |
| 1¹/₄ cups | 1¹/₂ cups | 2 cups | 2¹/₂ cups | 1³/₄ cups |
| 5 | 6 | 8 | 10 | 7 |
| 1¹/₄ cups | 1¹/₂ cups | 2 cups | 2¹/₂ cups | 1³/₄ cups |
| 2 hours | 2¹/₄ hours | 2¹/₂ hours | 3 hours | 2¹/₄ hours |

1 Grease and line base and sides of cake pan with one thickness of baking paper.

2 Sift flours, soda, spices and sugar into bowl. Add carrot, stir in combined oil, eggs and cream; do not over-mix. Spread mixture into pan.

3 Bake in moderate oven for time given in chart. Cover cake with foil halfway through baking if cake is over-browning.

4 Test cake by inserting a metal or wooden skewer into centre of cake; if cooked, skewer will come out clean, if there is moist cake mixture on skewer, return cake to oven for further 10 minutes before testing again.

5 Stand cake 15 minutes; turn onto wire rack to cool.

tip The cake will keep well for 5 days in an airtight container; or, it can be frozen for 3 months.

# *butter cake*

| INGREDIENTS | 12cm round | 15cm round<br>8cm x 17cm nut roll tin | 17cm round<br>15cm square<br>17cm octagonal | 20cm round | 22cm round<br>19cm square<br>9-cup pudding b<br>dolly varden tin |
|---|---|---|---|---|---|
| butter* | 60g | 100g | 125g | 185g | 250g |
| vanilla essence | 1/2 tsp | 3/4 tsp | 1 tsp | 1 1/2 tsp | 2 tsp |
| caster sugar | 1/3 cup | 1/2 cup | 3/4 cup | 1 cup | 1 1/2 cups |
| eggs* | 1 | 1 | 2 | 3 | 4 |
| SR flour | 3/4 cup | 1 1/4 cups | 1 1/2 cups | 2 1/4 cups | 3 cups |
| milk | 1/4 cup | 1/3 cup | 1/2 cup | 3/4 cup | 1 cup |
| baking time | 40 mins | 50 mins | 55 mins | 1 hour | 1 1/4 hours |

all cake pans to have straight sides (not sloping) except the pudding basin and dolly varden tin
* butter and eggs should be at room temperature for best results

spread cake mixture into prepared cake pan

insert skewer into cake to determine if it is cooked

1  Grease and line base and sides of cake pan with one thickness of baking paper.

2  Beat butter, essence and sugar in bowl with electric mixer until light and fluffy. Add eggs, one at a time, beating well between additions. Transfer mixture to larger bowl; stir in sifted flour and milk. Spread mixture into prepared pan.

3  Bake in moderate oven for time given in chart. Cover cake with foil halfway through baking if cake is over-browning.

4  Test cake by inserting a wooden or metal skewer into centre of cake; if cooked, skewer will come out clean, if there is moist cake mixture on the skewer, return cake to oven for further 10 minutes before testing again.

5  Stand cake 5 minutes; turn onto wire rack to cool.

tip  The cake will keep well for 2 days in an airtight container; or, it can be frozen for 3 months.

| 25cm round 23cm square | 28cm round 30cm heart 28cm x 34cm baking dish 26cm octagonal | 30cm round 28cm square | 30cm square | 24cm x 32cm oval |
| --- | --- | --- | --- | --- |
| 375g | 500g | 625g | 750g | 460g |
| 3 tsp | 1 tbs | 1 tbs | 1 tbs | 3 tsp |
| 2$^1/_2$ cups | 2$^1/_3$ cups | 3$^3/_4$ cups | 4$^1/_2$ cups | 2$^1/_3$ cups |
| 6 | 8 | 10 | 12 | 5 |
| 4$^1/_2$ cups | 6 cups | 7$^1/_2$ cups | 9 cups | 5$^3/_4$ cups |
| 1$^1/_2$ cups | 2 cups | 2$^1/_2$ cups | 3 cups | 1$^1/_2$ cups |
| 1$^1/_2$ hours | 1$^1/_2$ hours | 1$^3/_4$ hours | 2 hours | 1$^3/_4$ hours |

turn cake onto rack; use second rack to invert cake

# covering cakes

Cakes need to be covered with some sort of icing to stop them drying out, to preserve them and, of course, to make them look sensational.

Traditionally, and for preservation, a rich fruit cake should be used if the cake is to be kept for any length of time. In some cases, brides like to keep the top tier of a wedding cake to celebrate the first anniversary of marriage; in this event, a rich fruit cake must be used, and it must be covered with almond icing and then fondant. The almond icing imparts a lovely flavour to the cake and prevents the cake from staining the fondant.

Some people dislike the taste of almond icing; cakes can be covered with two layers of fondant. However, these cakes can only be kept for about 4 weeks.

You will need to make a sugar syrup which will adhere the almond icing and fondant to the cake. See sugar syrup recipe below.

All varieties of cake will usually keep quite well if covered completely in a soft icing such as vienna cream or a ganache. Since these icings are based on dairy products, the cakes should be covered and refrigerated. Refer to individual recipes for exact keeping times.

## sugar syrup

Sugar syrup is the easiest and cheapest ingredient to use for brushing over cakes.

$1/2$ cup (125ml) water
$1/2$ cup (110g) sugar
1 teaspoon glucose syrup

1 Combine ingredients in a small saucepan. Stir over high heat, without boiling, until sugar is dissolved. Bring to a boil, reduce heat; simmer, without stirring, 5 minutes, then cool to room temperature.

2 Store syrup in a jar, covered, at room temperature for up to 2 weeks.

## almond icing

Almond icing is easy to make, but can be bought ready-made from cake decorating suppliers, some health food shops, delicatessens and supermarkets. Marzipan meal can be used instead of almond meal, if preferred. Ideally, almond-icing-covered cakes need to stand for 1 day at room temperature before they are covered with fondant. This gives a manageable surface when applying the fondant.

$2^1/_3$ cups (375g) pure icing
    sugar, sifted
1 cup (125g) almond meal
2 tablespoons brandy
1 egg yolk
1 teaspoon lemon juice
pure icing sugar, extra

1 Combine icing sugar and almond meal in bowl, make well in centre, stir in brandy, egg yolk and lemon juice. When mixture becomes too stiff to stir, use hand to mix.

2 Knead lightly on surface dusted with sifted extra pure icing sugar.

3 Almond icing must be kept covered while not being handled, as exposure to air allows a crust to develop. Wrap tightly in plastic wrap and keep for up to 1 week in the refrigerator.

MAKES 500g

when ingredients become too stiff to stir, use hand to continue mixing

knead almond icing on surface dusted with a little sifted pure icing sugar

# how to cover a cake with almond icing

If necessary, trim top of cake/s with sharp knife to ensure it will sit flat when turned upside down.

Mix a little fondant and cold boiled water to a sticky paste. Spread about 2 tablespoons of this mixture into the centre of a sheet of baking or greaseproof paper about 5cm larger than the cake. Position cake on top.

Patching: Use a spatula or flexible knife blade and small pieces of almond icing to patch any holes in the surface of cake, both on the top and the sides.

Knead the almond icing gently until smooth, using a little extra sifted icing sugar to absorb stickiness.

Roll icing until it is about 7mm thick. Measure the sides of the cake, cut three or four strips large enough to fit the sides. Brush one side of each strip all over with sugar syrup. Attach the icing strips to the cake, sticky-side down. When covering a cake with right-angled corners, wrap the strips around the corners.

Use the base of the cake pan as a template to measure a piece of almond icing for the top of the cake.

Lift the top piece into place, and rub over the joins between pieces of icing to seal them together.

Leave cake standing on the paper to dry.

make a paste of fondant and water; use to secure cake to paper

patch surface of cake with almond icing; fill gap between cake and paper with almond icing

cover side/s of cake with neatly measured strips of rolled-out almond icing

with love, page 68

using cake pan as a guide, cut out piece of rolled-out almond icing for top of cake

position almond icing on cake; using fingers, gently mould edges together until smooth

## cake boards

We used a variety of boards for cakes in this book, but most of them were made from thick craft wood, painted the appropriate colours, then sealed to prevent the boards from staining. Traditionally, 5mm-thick plywood or masonite is used. It is important to cover cake boards neatly. There are many different materials available to use, such as paper, fabric, Contact plastic and fondant. Boards can be bought already covered in a variety of sizes from cake decorating suppliers and some craft shops.

When choosing boards for the upper tier/s of a cake, consider the size of the board carefully. A board that is too large will make the cake look heavy. As a rule, boards for upper tiers should be thinner and almost invisible. Make sure the underneath surface/s of the board/s are covered neatly.

Another attractive alternative is to use fondant to cover the board; the edge around the board can be covered with braid or ribbon.

to cover square board with paper, snip corners, glue in position

to cover with fondant, brush board with sugar syrup; cover with rolled-out fondant

to cover round board with paper, cut 5cm wider than board; snip, glue to board

to cover with fabric, cut fabric 5cm larger than board; use running stitch to pull tight

## *fondant*

Fondant-covered cakes need to be left to dry for at least 2 days, depending on the weather. Some cakes in this book need to be decorated with the fondant unset; others require it to be firm or completely set. Follow individual recipes.

2 tablespoons water
3 teaspoons gelatine
2 tablespoons glucose syrup
2 teaspoons glycerine
3 cups (480g) pure icing
   sugar, sifted
pure icing sugar, sifted, extra

1  Place the water in small saucepan, add gelatine; stir over low heat until gelatine is dissolved; do not boil. Remove from heat, stir in glucose syrup and glycerine; cool to warm.

2  Place icing sugar in large bowl, make well in centre, gradually stir in liquid. When mixture becomes too stiff to stir, mix with hand. Turn fondant onto surface that has been dusted with extra icing sugar. Knead lightly and gently until smooth, pliable and without stickiness.

MAKES 500g

make well in icing sugar; stir in liquid

knead fondant gently and lightly

# how to cover a cake with fondant

Brush sugar syrup lightly and evenly over cake (or over almond icing). Knead fondant with some pure icing sugar until smooth; roll fondant until it is about 7mm thick. Lift fondant onto cake with rolling pin. Smooth the fondant with hands dusted with icing sugar, ease the fondant around the sides and base of cake.

Push fondant in around the base; cut away excess fondant with a sharp knife.

Mix some scraps of fondant to a sticky paste with cold boiled water. You need about 2 tablespoons of this paste. Spread paste in the centre of the prepared board. Place cake on prepared board.

Move the cake to the correct position on the board; using a sharp Stanley knife, craft knife or scalpel, carefully cut away excess greaseproof paper around the base of the cake.

## PREPARED FONDANT

Prepared fondant can be bought from cake decorating suppliers, and some health food shops, delicatessens and supermarkets. There are several brands available – some are named "Soft Icing", "Prepared Icing" or "Ready to Roll Icing". All are easy to handle; simply knead the fondant gently, on a surface dusted with sifted pure icing sugar, until it is smooth. Then roll out fondant to the desired size and shape.

1 brush cake (in this case, covered with almond icing) with sugar syrup; cover cake with evenly-rolled-out fondant

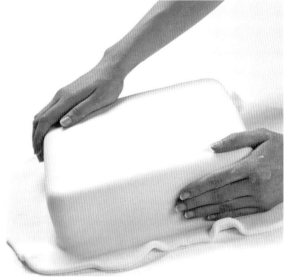

2 dust hands with icing sugar; gently ease fondant around corners and base of cake

3 use sharp knife or scalpel to neatly cut away excess fondant at base of cake

4 use paste of fondant and water to secure cake to board; neatly trim away excess paper with knife

# decorations

These simple tips will help you to secure ribbons and lace, and decorate cakes with flowers and candles, as preferred.

### SECURING RIBBONS, BRAID AND LACE

It is often easier to secure ribbon, braid and lace, etc, around the cake before the icing is set; it can be pulled quite tight and the ends joined neatly. As a general rule, ribbon ends can be held with pins and joined with egg white or sugar syrup, then the pins removed when the ends dry.

We used pins with large coloured heads for easy visibility and removal. Dressmakers' pins are easy to lose and must be avoided to prevent any nasty accidents.

decorative tools include cutters, wire, florist tape, and fresh and artificial flowers

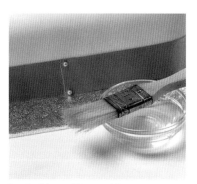

brush ribbon with egg white or sugar syrup; secure with pins, remove pins when dry

ribbons 'n' roses, page 24

### ARTIFICIAL FLOWERS

Artificial flowers can be used in different ways. They can be pulled from their stems and positioned in unset icing, or they can be wired and taped, with florist tape, to other flowers to make sprays or posies.

### FRESH FLOWERS

Fresh flowers look wonderful and can be arranged at home at the last minute, or you can have them arranged by a florist. In this case, collect them as late as possible and make sure you explain clearly to the florist how the flowers are to be arranged on the cake.

Keep any arrangements in the refrigerator. Make sure flowers are dry before they are placed on cake; drops of water will mark fondant.

Avoid pushing wired flowers into the cake, as it is extremely easy to cut through wire and cut it into small dangerous particles.

### FLORIST TAPE AND WIRE

These are used to hold flowers and ribbon in position. Always cover wire or flower stems with florist tape if they are to be inserted into icing or cake.

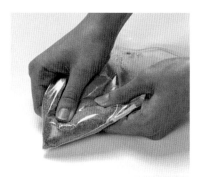

rub colouring through sugar enclosed in a strong plastic bag

### COLOURED SUGAR

Some coloured sugars can be bought in small jars from most supermarkets, however, it is simple to colour your own sugar. Use crystal or caster sugar, depending on the texture you prefer. Place the required amount of sugar in a plastic bag, add a tiny amount of colouring; work colouring through sugar by "massaging" plastic bag. Add more colouring as required. Sugar will keep in a jar indefinitely.

### CANDLES

The easiest way to fix candles to a cake is to push them into the fondant. Alternatively, buy plastic candle holders and push them into the fondant.

# modelling fondant

This fondant is best made a day before required, it can be frozen for four weeks.

2 teaspoons gelatine
1¹/₂ tablespoons water
2 teaspoons glucose syrup
1¹/₂ cups (240g) pure
    icing sugar, sifted

1  Sprinkle gelatine over the water in cup; stand cup in small saucepan of simmering water, stirring until gelatine is dissolved, add glucose.

2  Place half the icing sugar in medium bowl, stir in gelatine mixture. Gradually stir in remaining icing sugar, knead on surface dusted with extra sifted pure icing sugar until smooth and elastic. Wrap tightly in plastic wrap to prevent crust developing.

MAKES 250g

## equipment

### PIPING BAGS

Piping bags can be bought from cake decorating or chefs' suppliers; these are usually made from a waterproof fabric, and can have screws attached to hold icing tubes.

Bags can also be made from greaseproof or baking paper – these will hold various-shaped tubes, or the tips of the bags can be cut to the size you require. These are ideal for small amounts of icing.

Another option is to use a small plastic bag. Push the icing into the corner of the bag, twist the bag around the icing, snip the tip to the desired size and shape.

cut a square from paper, cut in half diagonally; hold apex of one triangle

twist first one point, then the other, into a cone shape; bring three points together

secure the three points with a staple; repeat with other triangle

### ICING TUBES

Tubes are made from metal or plastic, and can be bought from cake decorating suppliers, some craft shops, supermarkets and cookware shops.

### COLOURINGS

There are many varieties available: liquid, powder and paste. See glossary for further information.

Lustre colour is a powder available from cake decorating suppliers and craft shops in metallic shades, and is applied with a paintbrush. Though non-toxic, it's best to remove lustre-decorated items before serving.

### EXTRA EQUIPMENT

A ball tool is used to shape petals and flowers. It is available from cake decorating suppliers and some craft shops.

A candy thermometer measures the temperature of syrups. It is available from hardware and cookware shops.

Non-stick rolling pins are available from cake decorating and chefs' suppliers and cookware shops.

A craft knife or scalpel is useful for fine cutting and trimming work.

tools of the trade: a piping bag and a selection of metal and plastic icing tubes

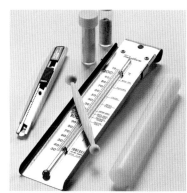

a craft knife, ball tool, lustre colours and a candy thermometer are all useful

## royal icing

1½ cups (240g) pure icing sugar, approximately
1 egg white
½ teaspoon lemon juice

1 Sift icing sugar through very fine sieve. Lightly beat egg white in small bowl with wooden spoon; add icing sugar, a heaped tablespoon at a time, beating well after each addition.

2 When icing reaches the desired consistency, add juice; beat well. Cover surface of icing tightly with plastic wrap while not using to prevent crust developing.

tip Small quantities of royal icing can be made using 1 teaspoon egg white. Mix in a cup with a teaspoon, adding enough pure icing sugar to give the desired consistency. Add a drop of lemon juice.

## vienna cream

Have butter and milk at room temperature for best results.

125g butter
1½ cups (240g) icing sugar mixture
2 tablespoons milk

Beat butter in small bowl with electric mixer until as white as possible. Gradually beat in half the icing sugar, milk, then remaining icing sugar.

## dark chocolate ganache

½ cup (125ml) cream
400g dark chocolate, chopped

Bring cream to a boil in small saucepan, pour over chocolate in small bowl, stirring until chocolate melts. Cover, refrigerate, stirring occasionally, about 30 minutes or until mixture is spreadable.

## white chocolate ganache

½ cup (125ml) cream
300g white chocolate, chopped

Bring cream to a boil in small saucepan; pour over chocolate in small bowl, stirring until chocolate melts. Cover, refrigerate, stirring occasionally, about 30 minutes or until mixture is spreadable.

vienna cream

white chocolate ganache

fluffy frosting

royal icing

dark chocolate ganache

## fluffy frosting

1 cup (220g) caster sugar
1/3 cup (80ml) water
2 egg whites

Combine sugar and the water in small saucepan; stir over heat, without boiling, until sugar is dissolved. Boil, uncovered, without stirring, until syrup reaches 116°C on candy thermometer or when a teaspoon of syrup, dropped into a cup of cold water, will form a soft ball when rolled between fingers. Remove from heat to allow bubbles to subside. Meanwhile, beat egg whites in small bowl with electric mixer until soft peaks form. While mixer is operating, add hot syrup in thin stream; beat on high speed about 10 minutes or until mixture is thick and cool.

## glossary

**almond**
KERNELS nuts with brown skin intact.
MEAL also known as ground almonds.
**bicarbonate of soda** also known as baking soda.
**butter** use salted or unsalted ("sweet") butter; 125g equals 1 stick of butter.
**cachous** small, round cake-decorating sweets available in various colours.

dolly varden tin

**chocolate**
DARK MELTS made from sugar, vegetable oil, cocoa, skim milk powder, butter oil, whey powder, emulsifier (soya lecithin), flavour and salt.
WHITE MELTS made from sugar, vegetable oil, whey powder and emulsifier (soya lecithin).
**clementine** a small citrus fruit, usually seedless, with a bittersweet flavour.
**coffee liqueur** use Tia Maria or Kahlua.
**colourings** available from cake decorating suppliers, some supermarkets and some craft shops; all are concentrated. Use a minute amount of any colouring first to determine its strength.
LIQUID the strength varies depending on the quality; useful for colouring most types of icings where pastel colours are needed.

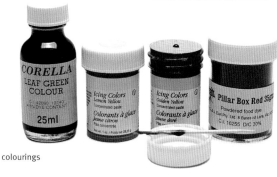

colourings

Large amounts of liquid colourings will dilute or break down most icings.
POWDERED these are edible and are used when primary colours or black are needed.
CONCENTRATED PASTES these are a little more expensive, but are the easiest to use and are suitable for pastel and bold colours.
**corn syrup** available in light or dark colour, either can be substituted for the other; glucose syrup (liquid glucose) can be substituted.
**cream**
SOUR (minimum fat content 35%) a thick, commercially cultured, soured cream.
THICKENED (minimum fat content 35%) a whipping cream containing a thickener.
**desiccated coconut** unsweetened, concentrated, dried shredded coconut.
**dolly varden tin** an almost-conical-shaped tin, mostly used for making cakes to represent a full skirt on a dressed doll.
**essence** also known as extracts.
flour
CORNFLOUR also known as cornstarch.
PLAIN an all-purpose flour, made from wheat.
SELF-RAISING plain (all-purpose) flour sifted with baking powder in the proportion of 1 cup flour to 2 teaspoons baking powder.
**fruit mince** also known as mince meat.
**gelatine** (gelatin) we used powdered gelatine; it is also available in sheet form, known as leaf gelatine.
**glucose syrup** also known as liquid glucose; a sugary syrup made from starches such as wheat and corn.

**glycerine** sweet colourless liquid, retains moisture in confectionery and is available from pharmacies.
**hazelnut meal** also known as ground hazelnuts.
**kaffir limes** and leaves wrinkle-skinned green fruit and aromatic leaves of a small citrus tree.
**jam** also known as preserve or conserve.
**marsala** a sweet fortified wine originally from Sicily.
**marzipan meal** made from ground apricot kernels; a less expensive substitute for almond meal.
**mascarpone** a fresh, thick, triple-cream cheese with a delicately sweet, slightly sour taste.

kaffir limes and leaves

**mixed peel** candied citrus peel.
**mixed spice** a blend of ground spices usually consisting of cinnamon, allspice and nutmeg.
**nutella** chocolate hazelnut spread.
**rind** also known as zest.
**rum** liquor made from fermented sugar cane; we used underproof rum.
**sugar** also known as crystal or table sugar.
BROWN a soft, granulated sugar retaining molasses for its characteristic colour.
CASTER also known as superfine or finely granulated table sugar.
ICING SUGAR MIXTURE also known as confectioners' or powdered sugar, it contains cornflour to keep it soft.
PURE ICING SUGAR also known as confectioners' sugar.
**sultanas** also known as golden raisins.
**vegetable oil** any of a number of oils sourced from plants.

# index

## measures

One Australian metric measuring cup holds approximately 250ml; one Australian metric tablespoon holds 20ml; one Australian metric teaspoon holds 5ml.

The difference between one country's measuring cups and another's is within a two- or three-teaspoon variance, and will not affect your cooking results. North America, New Zealand and the United Kingdom use a 15ml tablespoon.

All cup and spoon measurements are level. The most accurate way of measuring dry ingredients is to weigh them. When measuring liquids, use a clear glass or plastic jug with the metric markings.

We use large eggs with an average weight of 60g.

## dry measures

| METRIC | IMPERIAL |
|---|---|
| 15g | ½oz |
| 30g | 1oz |
| 60g | 2oz |
| 90g | 3oz |
| 125g | 4oz (¼lb) |
| 155g | 5oz |
| 185g | 6oz |
| 220g | 7oz |
| 250g | 8oz (½lb) |
| 280g | 9oz |
| 315g | 10oz |
| 345g | 11oz |
| 375g | 12oz (¾lb) |
| 410g | 13oz |
| 440g | 14oz |
| 470g | 15oz |
| 500g | 16oz (1lb) |
| 750g | 24oz (1½lb) |
| 1kg | 32oz (2lb) |

## liquid measures

| METRIC | IMPERIAL |
|---|---|
| 30ml | 1 fluid oz |
| 60ml | 2 fluid oz |
| 100ml | 3 fluid oz |
| 125ml | 4 fluid oz |
| 150ml | 5 fluid oz (¼ pint/1 gill) |
| 190ml | 6 fluid oz |
| 250ml | 8 fluid oz |
| 300ml | 10 fluid oz (½ pint) |
| 500ml | 16 fluid oz |
| 600ml | 20 fluid oz (1 pint) |
| 1000ml (1 litre) | 1¾ pints |

## length measures

| METRIC | IMPERIAL |
|---|---|
| 3mm | ⅛in |
| 6mm | ¼in |
| 1cm | ½in |
| 2cm | ¾in |
| 2.5cm | 1in |
| 5cm | 2in |
| 6cm | 2½in |
| 8cm | 3in |
| 10cm | 4in |
| 13cm | 5in |
| 15cm | 6in |
| 18cm | 7in |
| 20cm | 8in |
| 23cm | 9in |
| 25cm | 10in |
| 28cm | 11in |
| 30cm | 12in (1ft) |

## oven temperatures

These oven temperatures are only a guide for conventional ovens. For fan-forced ovens, check the manufacturer's manual.

| | °C (CELSIUS) | °F (FAHRENHEIT) | GAS MARK |
|---|---|---|---|
| Very slow | 120 | 250 | ½ |
| Slow | 150 | 275-300 | 1-2 |
| Moderately slow | 160 | 325 | 3 |
| Moderate | 180 | 350-375 | 4-5 |
| Moderately hot | 200 | 400 | 6 |
| Hot | 220 | 425-450 | 7-8 |
| Very hot | 240 | 475 | 9 |

# ARE YOU MISSING SOME COOKBOOKS?

*The Australian Women's Weekly* Cookbooks are available from bookshops, cookshops, supermarkets and other stores all over the world. You can also buy direct from the publisher, using the order form below.

| TITLE | RRP | QTY | TITLE | RRP | QTY |
|---|---|---|---|---|---|
| 100 Fast Fillets | £6.99 | | Grills | £6.99 | |
| After Work Fast | £6.99 | | Healthy Heart Cookbook | £6.99 | |
| A Taste of Chocolate | £6.99 | | Indian Cooking Class | £6.99 | |
| Beginners Cooking Class | £6.99 | | Japanese Cooking Class | £6.99 | |
| Beginners Thai | £6.99 | | Just For One | £6.99 | |
| Best Food Fast | £6.99 | | Just For Two | £6.99 | |
| Breads & Muffins | £6.99 | | Kids' Birthday Cakes | £6.99 | |
| Brunches, Lunches & Treats | £6.99 | | Kids Cooking | £6.99 | |
| Cafe Classics | £6.99 | | Kids' Cooking Step-by-Step | £6.99 | |
| Cafe Favourites | £6.99 | | Low-carb, Low-fat | £6.99 | |
| Cakes, Bakes & Desserts | £6.99 | | Low-fat Food for Life | £6.99 | |
| Cakes Biscuits & Slices | £6.99 | | Low-fat Meals in Minutes | £6.99 | |
| Cakes Cooking Class | £6.99 | | Main Course Salads | £6.99 | |
| Caribbean Cooking | £6.99 | | Mexican | £6.99 | |
| Casseroles | £6.99 | | Middle Eastern Cooking Class | £6.99 | |
| Casseroles & Slow-Cooked Classics | £6.99 | | Mince in Minutes | £6.99 | |
| Cheap Eats | £6.99 | | Moroccan & the Foods of North Africa | £6.99 | |
| Cheesecakes: baked and chilled | £6.99 | | Muffins, Scones & Breads | £6.99 | |
| Chicken | £6.99 | | New Casseroles | £6.99 | |
| Chicken Meals in Minutes | £6.99 | | New Curries | £6.99 | |
| Chinese & the foods of Thailand, Vietnam, Malaysia & Japan) | £6.99 | | New Finger Food | £6.99 | |
| | | | New French Food | £6.99 | |
| Chinese Cooking Class | £6.99 | | New Salads | £6.99 | |
| Christmas Cooking | £6.99 | | Party Food and Drink | £6.99 | |
| Chocs & Treats | £6.99 | | Pasta Meals in Minutes | £6.99 | |
| Cocktails | £6.99 | | Potatoes | £6.99 | |
| Cookies & Biscuits | £6.99 | | Quick & Simple Cooking (Apr 08) | £6.99 | |
| Cooking Class Cake Decorating | £6.99 | | Rice & Risotto | £6.99 | |
| Cupcakes & Fairycakes | £6.99 | | Sauces Salsas & Dressings | £6.99 | |
| Detox | £6.99 | | Sensational Stir-Fries | £6.99 | |
| Dinner Lamb | £6.99 | | Simple Healthy Meals | £6.99 | |
| Easy Comfort Food (Apr 08) | £6.99 | | Simple Starters, Mains & Puds | £6.99 | |
| Easy Curry | £6.99 | | Soup | £6.99 | |
| Easy Midweek Meals | £6.99 | | Stir-fry | £6.99 | |
| Easy Spanish-Style | £6.99 | | Superfoods for Exam Success | £6.99 | |
| Food for Fit and Healthy Kids | £6.99 | | Tapas Mezze Antipasto & other bites | £6.99 | |
| Foods of the Mediterranean | £6.99 | | Thai Cooking Class | £6.99 | |
| Foods That Fight Back | £6.99 | | Traditional Italian | £6.99 | |
| Fresh Food Fast | £6.99 | | Vegetarian Meals in Minutes | £6.99 | |
| Fresh Food for Babies & Toddlers | £6.99 | | Vegie Food | £6.99 | |
| Good Food for Babies & Toddlers | £6.99 | | Wicked Sweet Indulgences | £6.99 | |
| Great Kids' Cakes (Mar 08) | £6.99 | | Wok, Meals in Minutes | £6.99 | |
| Greek Cooking Class | £6.99 | | TOTAL COST: | £ | |

Mr/Mrs/Ms _____

Address_____ Postcode_____

Day time phone _____ email* (optional)_____

I enclose my cheque/money order for £ _____

or please charge £ _____

to my: ☐ Access ☐ Mastercard ☐ Visa ☐ Diners Club

Card number ☐☐☐☐ ☐☐☐☐ ☐☐☐☐ ☐☐☐☐

Expiry date _____ 3 digit security code *(found on reverse of card)* _____

Cardholder's name_____ Signature _____

**To order:** Mail or fax – photocopy or complete the order form above, and send your credit card details or cheque payable to: Australian Consolidated Press (UK), ACP Books, 10 Scirocco Close, Moulton Park Office Village, Northampton NN3 6AP. phone (+44) (0)1604 642200 fax (+44) (0)1604 642300 email books@acpuk.com or order online at www.acpuk.com

**Non-UK residents:** We accept the credit cards listed on the coupon, or cheques, drafts or International Money Orders payable in sterling and drawn on a UK bank. Credit card charges are at the exchange rate current at the time of payment.

**Postage and packing UK:** Add £1.00 per order plus £1.75 per book. **Postage and packing overseas:** Add £2.00 per order plus £3.50 per book.

All pricing current at time of going to press and subject to change/availability. **Offer ends 31.12.2008**

\* By including your email address, you consent to receipt of any email regarding this magazine, and other emails which inform you of ACP's other publications, products, services and events, and to promote third party goods and services you may be interested in.

**TEST KITCHEN**
**Food director** Pamela Clark
**Associate food editor** Alexandra Somerville

**ACP BOOKS**
**General manager** Christine Whiston
**Editorial director** Susan Tomnay
**Creative director** Hieu Chi Nguyen
**Designer** Hannah Blackmore
**Director of sales** Brian Cearnes
**Marketing manager** Bridget Cody
**Business analyst** Ashley Davies
**Operations manager** David Scotto
**International rights enquires** Laura Bamford
lbamford@acpuk.com

**acp** books

ACP Books are published by ACP Magazines a division of PBL Media Pty Limited
**Group publisher, Women's lifestyle**
Pat Ingram
**Director of sales, Women's lifestyle**
Lynette Phillips
**Commercial manager, Women's lifestyle**
Seymour Cohen
**Marketing director, Women's lifestyle**
Matthew Dominello
**Public relations manager, Women's lifestyle**
Hannah Deveraux
**Creative director, Events, Women's lifestyle**
Luke Bonnano
**Research Director, Women's lifestyle**
Justin Stone
**ACP Magazines, Chief Executive officer**
Scott Lorson
**PBL Media, Chief Executive officer**
Ian Law

**Produced by** ACP Books, Sydney.
**Published by** ACP Books, a division of ACP Magazines Ltd, 54 Park St, Sydney; GPO Box 4088, Sydney, NSW 2001. phone (02) 9282 8618 fax (02) 9267 9438. acpbooks@acpmagazines.com.au www.acpbooks.com.au
**Printed by** Dai Nippon in Korea.

**Australia** Distributed by Network Services, phone +61 2 9282 8777 fax +61 2 9264 3278 networkweb@networkservicescompany.com.au
**United Kingdom** Distributed by Australian Consolidated Press (UK), phone (01604) 642 200 fax (01604) 642 300 books@acpuk.com
**New Zealand** Distributed by Netlink Distribution Company, phone (9) 366 9966 ask@ndc.co.nz
**South Africa** Distributed by PSD Promotions, phone (27 11) 392 6065/6/7 fax (27 11) 392 6079/80 orders@psdprom.co.za
**Canada** Distributed by Publishers Group Canada phone (800) 663 5714 fax (800) 565 3770 service@raincoast.com

Cooking class cake decoration: the Australian women's weekly.
Includes index.
ISBN 978 186396 726 6 (pbk.).
1. Cake decorating. I. Clark, Pamela.
II. Title : Australian women's weekly.
641.86539
© ACP Magazines Ltd 2008
ABN 18 053 273 546
This publication is copyright. No part of it may be reproduced or transmitted in any form without the written permission of the publishers.
First published in 2000 as *Celebration Cakes*. Revised and updated 2008.

Send recipe enquiries to:
recipeenquiries@acpmagazines.com.au